His Military Commanders

The Brilliant Military Strategies of Hannibal, Alexander The Great, Sun Tzu, Julius Caesar, Napoleon Bonaparte, And 30 Other Historical Commanders

By Barry Linton

Table of Contents

Foreword

For as long as mankind has existed there has been war. In times of dire need, turmoil, and opportunity great leaders and warriors throughout history have heeded the call of battle. Those in positions of leadership often exhibit many admirable traits, usually creating a stark contrast with their shortcomings. The famous leaders featured in this book are varied individuals, some thrust into their leadership roles by necessity and circumstance while others were driven by ambition and even blood lust. While many are set apart by over 1000 years of history, each shared the inherent potential to inspire and aspire to greater deeds.

Combat has changed radically through the centuries, bringing new technological innovations as well as many socioeconomic and political changes. Rather than leading from the front lines, it is now possible for a general to issue commands from thousands of miles away. Such battlefield advances are commonplace now but were utterly unheard of in the time of Caesar. Early in the history of mankind, it was necessary and preferred for leaders to take charge in the worst conditions at the front with their soldiers and lead them to victory. Regardless of the time that has passed, the leaders focused upon in this book show many defining qualities, such as courage under fire and the willingness to fight for their beliefs. Some chose to become heroes, others tyrants, and some sought only to fulfill their duty.

Alexander the Great, Hannibal Barca, Julius Caesar – these are some of the greatest military minds in recorded history. Their battles and tactics has been the subject of study and provided valuable lessons to aspiring tacticians and leaders throughout the ages.

Chapter 1: Leaders of the Ancient World

Sun Tzu

Born: 544 B.C.E.

Died: 496 B.C.E.

Military General and Tactician

Sun Tzu was a Chinese tactician, philosopher, and military general who is known primarily as the author of the treatise, The Art of War. The life of Sun Tzu is shrouded in mystery, with few surviving accounts to tell his tale. Historians have faced conflicting accounts that blurred the line between fact and fiction. What is known however is that as a younger man he served King Ho-Lu of Wu, and brought great success as his general and strategist. His battlefield victories for the Wu built a reputation that would only grow with time. In 506 BC, Sun Tzu commanded the Wu army at the battle of Boju. He faced a numerically superior army of

200,000 with only 30,000 men. The battle would not be won by the Wu using brute strength, but through careful placement of his soldiers, personal initiative, and understanding the enemy. The enemy Chu army devised a plan in which one contingent would take defensive positions on the far side of the river, and the other would block the Wu army's escape route before converging from both directions. Through careful collection of intelligence, the Wu forces determined that the enemy general Nang was cruel and disliked by his men. When Nang attacked early, Sun Tzu attacked in force when the enemy had only crossed halfway. Nang's men were slaughtered midstream and their already low morale resulted in a rout. Sun Tzu attacked in his opponent's vulnerable spots, used a bottleneck to prevent his enemy from massing full strength, and then continued to pursue the fleeing opponents. They were defeated in five further engagements and eventually the Wu army and King Ho-Lu captured the Chu capital of Ying.

Sun Tzu believed in psychological dominance, based upon a superior knowledge of the enemy. He employed tactics that would harm enemy morale, including surprise or guerrilla attacks when the enemy least expected it. His teachings grew to become the most famous of China's seven Military Classic writings and were especially influential during the Warring States period of China. For many hundreds of years his treatise was required reading for many soldiers and officers in China. In time, the Art of War spread across the globe and was read by such famous leaders as Mao Zedong, Oda Nobunaga, and General Douglas MacArthur. His tactics and philosophies are repeatedly employed throughout history and many are made note of in this book.

Alexander the Great
Born: 356 B.C.E.

Died: 323 B.C.E.

King of Macedon and Emperor of Persia

Alexander is considered by most modern historians to be the most successful military leader of all time. He came to be known as a King, an Emperor, and even was worshiped by some as a God. Alexander of Macedon conquered and expanded an Empire extending from Greece to faraway Indian Asia in a life cut short at the age of only 32. His father, Philip the Second, had taken particular care to ensure that he was well versed in war at an early age. In the key battle of Chaeronea – a decisive encounter in Phillip's campaign to defeat the Greeks and add their lands to the Macedonian Empire – the 18-year-old Alexander was given the responsibility of commanding the left wing in the line of battle. Even at this age, his military genius shone through and he was the first to break through the enemy's lines. He fought bravely and was seen as a great credit to his father.

Alexander shared the ambitions of his father and sought to invade the Persian Empire. After ensuring that his homelands of Macedonia were secured and provisions made, he campaigned in the Balkans and Greece to defeat all further enemy opposition at home before leaving abroad for Asia.

Alexander was an inspirational leader of men, set apart by his ability to motivate even under the harshest of conditions. An account recorded by the Roman historian Plutarch describes an event during the forced desert march where some of his soldiers brought Alexander their meager water supply in an upturned helmet. Alexander without hesitation refused to drink, boldly declaring that he would suffer thirst alongside his men. The surrounding soldiers were moved and responded that they would "follow such a King anywhere". Alexander thoroughly understood the effectiveness of such well-timed public gestures in securing the support of his men when conditions were challenging. He made special effort to make the ordinary soldier feel that he identified with their hardships. He also strove to fill them with pride by cultivating an image of himself as a calm, collected, and charismatic leader. He has also been described as taking special care with trust and morale building gestures after battles, often conducting elaborate special funeral ceremonies in honor of fallen troops and distributing riches and other plunder to those warriors who distinguished themselves in combat. The fact that he carried his own fair share of wounds gave greater force to this bond that he shared with his soldiers. One historian wrote that his men declared their dedication to him and that they would not regard themselves as "weary, or thirsty, or as mortals at all, so long as they had such a King".

Alexander's most confident and natural place in combat was leading at the front of his favored Macedonian cavalry unit. His distinctive style of command – leading from the front – was taught early and reinforced to him by his father. The ruler of Macedonia was required to prove his worth to rule the kingdom and the greater world.

This was accomplished by demonstrating his dominance to his followers with the evidence of his considerable fighting skill. But Alexander's brash nature went beyond this basic tenet. Every time he led a charge across the field of battle to attack an enemy head-on, Alexander seriously endangered his army's most valuable asset: himself. Historians have often criticized Alexander for his overly aggressive nature that culminated in unnecessary risk-taking, but these faults are sometimes excused considering his relative youth and temperament.

Alexander also recognized the efficiency of psychological warfare. He recognized that confidence and boldness usually trumped an overcautious enemy. Shocking and surprising his opponent was a key component of his tactics, and he often left opponents reeling with his surprising speed and unrelenting aggression. Alexander never hesitated to use maximum force to win the day and achieve total victory. He held no special respect for human life and made no attempts to avoid collateral damage. He would typically only show mercy when it was politically advantageous, and terror was also an important part of his arsenal. His military campaigns in the Indus Valley in 325 B.C.E. have been characterized by some historians as genocide. Alexander probably viewed this as a suitable punishment for those who resisted his conquest, and also as a practical means of enforcing his rule. Alexander's infamous destruction of the rebellious city of Thebes was only the first of many examples in which Alexander ruthlessly used terror and fear to deter potential revolt.

By 334 B.C.E. he was ready to cross the Hellespont into Persian-ruled Anatolia, heading an army consisting of some 40,000 infantry and 5,000 cavalry. The expedition was carefully and expertly prepared. Alexander ordered his support and supply ships to shadow the army's movement along the coast. This was advantageous because it allowed heavy siege equipment to keep up with the speed of his advance. In one particular skirmish, Alexander encountered an army assembled by the local Persian magistrate. Alexander personally and recklessly led the cavalry charge across the river. He was quickly surrounded by his enemies and was nearly killed in the melee. Ultimately however, his boldness and initiative overcame and won the day. The success and future of the expedition looked very uncertain for a time, especially so given that the Greek cities of Western Anatolia were less than enthusiastic about being "liberated" by Alexander's conquering army. Meanwhile, the Persian forces delivered a deadly strategic counter-attack, employing Greek mercenaries to charge along the Aegean into Greece and toward his homeland of Macedonia itself.

When Alexander's army finally arrived and marched into Syria in the dead of winter in 333 B.C.E., it was perfectly reasonable for the Persian Emperor Darius to believe that Alexander's army was falling into a trap. Darius's much larger force was marching westward to crush their incursion. Alexander was prepared and confident that if he could bring the enemy army to battle, he would swiftly defeat them. The two armies finally met on a plain. The two generals adopted opposite postures with Darius focusing purely on defenses, while Alexander boldly launched an all-out attack. Alexander once again aggressively led his cavalry in person, and collided into the unprepared Persian left flank. Darius immediately fled to avoid the humiliation of capture at the hands of his greatest enemy. On that decisive day, his army was completely smashed to pieces. With no significant opposition left to stop his March, the entirety of the Eastern Mediterranean opened up to Alexander's goals of conquest. Upon arriving in Egypt, he was greeted as and believed to be the next ruling Pharaoh. If he were a lesser man, these accomplishments might have swayed him from pressing forward. Alexander thought only of his dream to completely dominate the Persian lands. He again met Darius in battle at

Gaugamela, and once more used his Macedonian cavalry to achieve victory against the numerically superior Persian army.

Alexander pressed his campaign further to the east, assuming supreme dominion over the remaining Persian Empire provinces. The relationship with his followers grew tenuous as he achieved greater and greater successes. His style of leadership had always been such that he would never ask his men to do what he was not willing to do himself. He stood and fought shoulder to shoulder and shield to shield with his trusted companions, and made an effort to dine among them. This style of leadership made the senior members of his army uneasy because it exposed him to unnecessary risk, and by extent risked the future of the Army.

He claimed to have descended from the famed demigod Heracles, as well as the legendary Trojan War hero Achilles. Yet there was infighting among his men, plots, and even attempts at mutiny. Alexander did not hesitate to have his second in command executed for mutiny and later killed another close companion in a drunken feud between the two former friends.

Nothing quenched Alexander's thirst for adventure and military conquest. In 326 B.C.E. he finally reached and invaded northern India. Using his significant tactical acumen, he managed to overcome fierce resistance at the battle of Hydaspes. Alexander learned firsthand the great danger of fighting war elephants and learned to counter them. The death toll resulting from the battle proved catastrophic and Alexander's army refused to follow him further into India. With morale low, Alexander was forced to lead his army back along the sea. Alexander suffered a severe wound leading an attack near the river Hydraoates. He finally arrived back in Persia in 325 B.C.E. after a costly and ill advised desert march.

Alexander's spirit remained unbroken and full of plans for new incursions into Arabia and

North Africa. Years of fighting had finally taken its toll. Alexander carried the wounds of his military career. Finally, Alexander's body succumbed to an aggressive fever. He died at the palace of Nebuchadnezzar II in Babylon, leaving his ambitions unfulfilled and empire with no heir.

Pyrrhus of Epirus
Born: 319 B.C.E.

Died: 272 B.C.E.

King of Epirus and Adventurer

Pyrrhus of Epirus was a Greek adventurer who fought primarily for wealth and power in the Mediterranean world that had been left unstable after the era of Alexander. When he was a young man, he took part in the power struggles and battles between Alexander's successors – the Macedon Antigonids as well as the Ptolemies of Egypt – and had no qualms of switching sides if it suited his interests. He campaigned in Greece where he eventually was established as King of a small state called Epirus. This helped to create a reputation that traveled far. In 81 B.C.E., Pyrrhus was asked by a small Greek city in southern Italy called Tarentum to help defend it against the aggressions of the Romans. Their expansionist Republic was threatening the independence of many of the cities in that region. Rome was not yet a mighty empire, and it is likely that Pyrrhus sensed an opportunity for easily gained victories and the benefit of conquest.

He finally arrived in Tarentum B.C.E. with 25,000 infantry and 20 elephants. While these animals were already commonplace in cities and combat farther east, to this point they were previously uncommon and largely unknown in Italy. Initially, the strength of his cavalry and the shock effect of his elephants led him to an early and comfortable victory over the Romans at the nearby battle of Heraclea. But in the following year at Asculum, he achieved victory only through the massive loss of human life. This is the battle that is associated with his namesake. It later came to be called, "Pyrrhic victory".

At this point, Pyrrhus took a break from his conquest of Rome and accepted a new invitation. The Greek city of Sicily requested his aid in fighting against the Carthaginians. The campaign on the island lasted for three years and by the end he had proclaimed himself King of Sicily. What he failed to accomplish however was to demolish the most staunchly defended Carthaginian strongholds. His dictatorial policies also alienated local populations. Despite these failings, Hannibal is said to have described Pyrrhus as second only to Alexander the Great as a military commander. In 75 B.C.E., he finally returned to Southern Italy to resume his war against Rome. At Beneventum, he only managed to achieve a draw. His elephants no longer had the shock value they initially did, and the Romans were prepared to counter them. When he became short of money and soldiers, Pyrrhus would return to Greece. Once again sensing an opportunity, he seized the throne of Macedon.

His military campaigns were brought to an abrupt and inglorious end during riots and fighting in the city of Argos. An old woman dropped a heavy stone tile from a rooftop upon the head of Pyrrhus. A soldier then severed his unconscious head from his shoulders. Pyrrhus of Epirus – whose military career was characterized by seizing and exploiting opportunities – was undone in a single moment of misfortune.

Darius the Third
Born: Unknown

Died: 330 B.C.E.

Persian King

There are times when normally competent military commanders are truly outmatched by the opponents they encounter. There is no doubt that this is the case for Darius III, who was soundly defeated at the hands of the military prodigy, Alexander of Macedon. His defeat sounded the end of Persia as a globe spanning and dominant empire. Appearing primarily in Greek written texts, Darius has inevitably been presented through the ages in a negative light, yet there is strong evidence at least for his stalwart courage. As a young man he distinguished himself in single combat against a Champion sent forward by an Iranian mountain tribe in rebellion against the Persian Empire.

His route to the Persian throne was difficult and winding, for he was only a minor noble of the royal family, posted far away from the center of the empire as Governor of Armenia. A series of traitorous poisonings engineered by the palace court wiped out the majority of the ruling elite, paving the road to his Imperial rule in 336 B.C.E.

When Alexander initially invaded the Anatolian Empire in 334 B.C.E., Darius could be excused for treating this as a local difficulty to be handled by the regional governors. When he eventually did respond to the invasion and

advanced with his army into Syria in 333 B.C.E.,
he seemed to have outmaneuvered Alexander
into a disadvantageous position. Darius
converged behind the Macedonians on the
coastal plain. There he gathered his army into a
strong defensive position, then tried an
outflanking move – tactics that might have
succeeded against a lesser opponent. The Persian
forces were quickly shattered by Macedonian
cavalry, however, and Darius was forced to flee
the battlefield to avoid capture and greater
losses. Darius's second great battle against
Alexander proved to be just as disastrous.
Fleeing back to the city of Ecbatana, Darius
intended to raise another army to continue the
fight, but a rebellious subordinate governor
captured him, held him prisoner for a time, and
finally killed him.

Alexander the Great vs Darius III

After his humiliating defeat at the hands
of Alexander in 333 B.C.E., the Persian ruler
Darius III, was resolute in his decision to fight

the Macedonians again and crush them. He assembled a considerable army by calling upon tribute and reserves from his Asian provinces, and then waited in Mesopotamia for Alexander to come to him. In the summer of 331 BC, Alexander – equally eager for yet another clash – marched from Egypt through Syria to the Euphrates River. Darius used the quickness of his cavalry to deny them supplies and shelter in the Euphrates valley, forcing Alexander to continue marching his army northeast to the Tigris River. Darius waited patiently for his rival Alexander's much smaller army on the far side of the river.

Alexander crossed the Tigris unaware of the disposition or strength of Darius's gathered army. After four days of marching along the river, Alexander managed to take prisoners in a clash with Persian cavalry. Interrogation revealed that Darius was waiting with his army on a plain some 6 miles away, using intervening hills to block line of sight. Alexander fortified his own camp and then spent four days preparing for the battle to come. Late on the evening of September 29, he advanced his army en masse toward Guagamela with the intent of attacking at dawn after the night march. After finally reaching the crest of the hill above the Persian camp on the plain below, Alexander ordered his army to halt. After beholding the full scale of his enemy Darius's army, Alexander decided to wait. The following day, he surveyed the battlefield and finalized his battle plan. After deciding against the night attack, he made adjustments to his usual battle dispositions – his infantry phalanx would remain in the center, the companion cavalry would gather on the right, supported by a light cavalry left-wing. He also prepared measures in case of other possible battlefield developments. On the wings of his army, additional cavalry and skirmishers would be in position to counter any outflanking moves. He also stationed a second line of infantry in the rear of the line of battle, leaving them ready to turn around and defend the backs of the front line. Thus satisfactorily prepared, Alexander slept peacefully through the night. The following morning he marched his eager army down onto the plain of battle, riding as usual at the head of the Macedonian cavalry with the support of the best of his combat infantry. He led his entire army to the right, across the front of the waiting Persian lines. Alexander attacked the Persian left with his cavalry, while the unprepared Persian cavalry attempted outflanking moves but were soundly defeated. Obscured among the chaotic sounds of combat, with large plumes of dust rising from the dryness of the plain, Darius could not see Alexander's next move. Alexander the Great charged his heavy cavalry - with infantry support - to strike at Darius in the Persian army center. Taken completely by surprise, the Persian king fled. Alexander's initial instinct was to pursue him, but his horsemen were still needed to aid his other forces engaged in heated combat on other parts of the battlefield. The Persian army was soon scattered after suffering massive casualties. Alexander's victory was swift and indisputable.

Scipio Africanus
Born: 236 B.C.E.

Died: 183 B.C.E.

Roman General

Publius Cornelius Scipio was the true name of the man known as Scipio Africanus. He was the Roman commander who was key in winning the Second Punic war. He was only 17 years old when the war began and he fought in an army commanded by his father. His father was also named Publius Cornelius Scipio, and they both fought in the opening river skirmish of Hannibal's Italian campaign. He managed to make it through the battle of Cannae entirely unscathed, distinguishing himself in the rallying of survivors despite the overall Roman failure.

His military career remained overshadowed by his father until the elder Publius was killed in 211 B.C.E. while on campaign in Iberia. Scipio then took over his father's command under unfavorable circumstances, for the likelihood of Roman success in Spain was extremely low. In just four short years, he completely and utterly drove the Carthaginian forces from their strongholds in Iberia.

Scipio was a bold and charismatic leader, well-liked by his men and respected by his enemies. It was this boldness that led him to launch speedy attacks to keep his Carthaginian enemies at a disadvantage. In a surprise assault, he took their main base of operations at New Carthage. He followed up this victory with another victory against Hannibal's brother Hasdrubal. The Carthaginians responded to this loss by sending reinforcements into the region of southern Spain. This led to the major battle of Ilipa in 206 B.C.E., widely considered to be the height of Scipio's tactical prowess.

Both armies consisted of a wide variety of troop types from around the region. Standard battlefield procedure was for both generals to arrange their battle lines so that like fought like. Scipio turned this paradigm on its head, unexpectedly switching his formidable Legion infantry from the center to the wings where they would face the Carthaginian's least effective soldiers. Maneuvering his soldiers with considerable skill, his veteran legionary troops smashed the weaker Carthaginian line and then immediately moved inward from the flanks.

With Iberia finally conquered, Scipio then returned to Rome and would receive a hero's welcome. He was elected Consul and given permission to lead an army into Africa, where he planned to put pressure on Carthage. Crossing into Tunisia, he took up defensive positions outside the city and refused to be driven away or scattered. This forced Hannibal to return from Italy and led him to his defeat at the battle of Zama, finally forcing the Carthaginians to sue for peace with Rome.

Zama was the climactic battle of the Second Punic War and was fought in Tunisia. It was Scipio's scorched-earth tactics that forced Hannibal to return and defend. Despite having many new and hastily trained recruits, Scipio enjoyed a great deal of success likely due to his superior leadership. Hannibal tried to break the Roman defensive lines using his war elephants, but the legionaries were instructed to make gaps in the line and let them pass through. The Roman infantry then swarmed while the cavalry swept through the wings, smashing the Carthaginian opposition. When the horsemen returned to attack the Carthaginian flank, the battle was decisively won for Rome.

Aside from aiding his brother Lucius in the defeat of Antiochus III of Syria in 190 B.C.E., Scipio carried out no further recorded military actions of note.

Background: Roman Military

Rome developed one of the most efficient fighting forces in the Ancient World. Its Army evolved from light citizen militia into regular professional soldiers of the Legion. High Command was mostly entrusted to aristocratic amateurs – powerful politicians but only part-time soldiers, often without the necessary training or much in the way of military experience. Despite this haphazard system, commanders as inspired as Scipio Africanus and Julius Caesar emerged in the course of Rome's endlessly deadly warfare against enemies ranging from Carthaginians to Parthians to Celtic tribal warriors. Roman commanders did not typically lead from the front in the reckless manner of Alexander of Macedon, but they did generally share most of the risks and hardships of their men. Emperor Constantius, in 355 CE wrote that a Commander should inspire by example without being rash. He should go forward as a brave man to lead other brave men.

Commanders directed sieges and engineering works in person, as well as carrying out the essential religious functions of sacrifice and the reading of omens. In battle their position was just behind the front line, ready to intervene when troops needed encouragement or support. The general's chief duty was to show himself to those in danger, give praise it is due, threaten the cowardly, encourage the lazy, and bring aid to the wearied. Tenacity was probably the most striking quality of Roman leaders. A commander may be forgiven for losing the battle after an honorable fight, but he was expected to regroup his forces and renew the campaign until he eventually won.

The close bond that often developed between Roman legionaries and their immediate commander - rather than the Central Government - was one of the causes of the repeated coups and civil wars that scarred Roman history. Power in the Republic and the Empire ultimately rested with the Roman Legions. Tactically, Roman armies were limited to a small range of battlefield maneuvers drilled into the troops, enlivened by the occasional ambush. Discipline was mostly excellent and lower-level officers could be trusted to display resolve and initiative. Engineering skills were at a premium, seen in the construction of roads and defensive fortifications all across the Empire in both peace and war, as well as in siege works on campaign. Strategically the Romans were bold and aggressive in their expansionist phase, making ample use of terror to ensure the submission of their enemies. At a later stage they adopted the subtle diplomatic approach, as they became dependent on alliances and the incorporation of barbarian troops and other fighting forces. The enemies the Romans encountered – when not fighting one another – were varied indeed. In the third century B.C.E. the Carthaginians, based in North Africa, challenged the rising Roman Republic in the Punic Wars, a conflict that began as a contest for control of Sicily and ended as a fight to the death between two civilizations. Extending its power next into the eastern Mediterranean, Rome proved its superiority to the states that had succeeded Alexander's Empire. In Western Europe – Celtic and Germanic tribes put up stiff resistance to Rome, inflicting the occasional severe defeat. With mounting incursions by migrating Goths, Vandals, and the fierce Huns, the Western Roman Empire was eventually put under impossible strain.

Hannibal Barca
Born: 247 B.C.E.

Died: 182 B.C.E.

Carthaginian General

Hannibal Barca was trained in the art of warfare from an early age. He learned military wisdom and tactics primarily from his father, Hamilcar Barca. In his youth he also fought in the Carthaginian campaigns in Spain, giving him actual battlefield experience as the basis of his military foundation. He eventually inherited supreme leadership of the Carthaginian Army while in Spain in 21 B.C.E.

Roman sources also indicate that he inherited his father's burning desire for revenge after Carthage's defeat by Rome in the first Punic war.

It is unknown whether or not Hannibal deliberately intended to provoke war with Rome when he attacked the city of Saguntum in 219 BC. It is evident however that the following invasion of Italy was well prepared, with the route leading across Gaul and over the Alps scouted in advance. Hannibal easily took the Romans by surprise – Roman leaders assumed that he would stay in Spain and passively await their counterattack.

The journey across the Alps was extremely hazardous to both himself and his men. Hannibal's army was frequently attacked along the way by small local tribes who would engage him in skirmishes. Crossing the treacherous Alps was tough for men and animals, especially for Hannibal's signature war elephants who were unaccustomed to the cold. Only a fraction of the forces he initially left Spain with finally reached northern Italy.

The quality of Hannibal's Numidian horsemen was soon proven in the first clash in Italy, when they drove the Roman cavalry into a full retreat. Hannibal's charismatic personality and winning aura drew many to his army, and soon local Celtic tribesmen flocked to join his forces.

Hannibal's forces in Italy were drawn from a wide variety of mercenaries from Carthage's North African allies and also tributary states from and around Spain. Each group had their own unique specialty and purpose in Hannibal's battle plans. His forces consisted of tough and resilient Libyan foot soldiers, skilled Numidian horsemen armed with javelins and spears, and Spanish hill tribesmen armed with deadly yet distinctive short shorts. This broad multicultural army was united by common allegiance to its charismatic and talented general. He was supported by a number of lieutenants drawn from the Carthaginian aristocracy back home, including many of Hannibal's own relatives and friends.

Seeing the growing threat of his forces, the Romans sought to stamp out this invasion before it could proceed any further. They shifted an army north to block and confront Hannibal at the Trebia River, but the Roman leaders soon showed themselves to be tactically naive and too optimistic.

Hannibal led them into an attack across the river, then crushed the wings of their defensive formation with his heavy cavalry. Previously concealed troops soon emerged to strike the advancing Romans in their exposed flanks. This forced the Roman legionary infantry to fight their way through Hannibal's center and abandon the battlefield to avoid the impending massacre. The Romans failed to learn from this tactical disaster. The following year, Hannibal moved his army rapidly south into Etruria. For a second time, the Roman army hurried north to confront him in battle. Hannibal knew they were coming and selected the perfect site for an ambush, where the road passed between steep hills by the shore of Lake Trasimene.

There Hannibal's army faced a much larger force of eight legions led by the Roman consuls Lucius Aemilius Paulus and Gaius Terentius Varro. The Romans needed no urging to engage in battle, confident that they were strong enough to defeat Hannibal. On the morning of August 2nd, the Roman forces crossed the river and took up a defensive position between the river and high ground. Although Hannibal could see that this might prevent his superior cavalry from outflanking the Roman line, he decided to cross the river and then formed his army for combat. Hannibal knew that the Romans would attempt to win the battle in the center through the strength of their legionary infantry. He saw that this tactic offered the potential to spring a devastating trap. Opposite of the legionaries he positioned the

Spanish and Gallic foot soldiers – fierce tribal fighters but no match for the Romans – and sent them into close combat. On each flank of these lightly clad troops he placed his tough and disciplined Libyan infantry, who were wearing Roman style armor and marching in dense formation.

The Roman infantry fought a path forward into the Carthaginian center, where Hannibal had positioned himself. The opposing heavy cavalry fought on the wing next to the river, while the Carthaginians under his brother broke through to the Roman rear. On the other wing, Hannibal's swift and lightly armored Numidian horseman chased the cavalry of Rome's Italian allies from the battlefield. The Roman forces still appeared to be winning the battle in the center, but as the legionaries press forward, Hannibal ordered his Libyans to turn inward and squeeze the now disorganized and outnumbered Roman infantry from the flanks. The legions were already being crushed by this attack when Hannibal's devastating cavalry charged into the rear of their formation, completing a dreaded double envelopment. Few Romans escaped the massacre that followed.

Hannibal's tactics in this battle rank among the best in recorded history. They would continue to be admired and studied by other great military leaders throughout history. Ultimately the Romans marched foolishly into a trap and were massacred as Hannibal's army rushed down from the heights, pinning them against the lake with no means of retreat.

After this crushing defeat, Fabius Cunctator took charge, and immediately set to change the tactics of engaging the Carthaginians. By refusing to be drawn into lopsided battles, Fabius left Hannibal with the unenviable task of keeping his army and war animals supplied with food and fodder for an extended period of time in hostile territory. At the end of the campaigning season, Hannibal faced being trapped for the winter on a desolate plain that his troops had already stripped bare of resources. He escaped only by slipping past Fabius and his army in the middle of the night, reportedly creating an effective diversion using cattle with torches tied to their horns.

In the summer of 216 B.C.E. Hannibal and the Roman leadership – by this point eager for battle – engaged at Cannae. This battle proved to be the greatest triumph of Hannibal's career, but its aftermath has puzzled historians, for Hannibal made no effort to occupy the city of Rome even though it lay open and vulnerable to attack. From that point onward, Hannibal's campaign lost its clarity of purpose. He had achieved his and his father's original objective: the humiliating defeat of Rome. When the Romans would refuse to make peace, Hannibal was left to campaign around southern Italy for years. He would make alliances, capture and lose cities, win several decisive battles, and somehow managed to keep his army united.

The last opportunity for decisive victory was lost when his brother Hasdrubal was killed in northern Italy at the battle of Metaurus. Afterward, his head was thrown into Hannibal's camp. In 203 B.C.E., after 16 years in Italy, Hannibal was recalled to defend Carthage against the Roman invasion. He faced Scipio Africanus and his army of new recruits, alongside his former Numidian cavalry who were now fighting for the Romans. Hannibal was defeated, and Carthage was again forced to make peace on humiliating terms.

Hannibal spent the remainder of his life fleeing Roman capture and revenge around the Mediterranean. Hannibal eventually chose suicide rather than submit to Roman captivity.

Julius Caesar

Born: July 13, 100 B.C.E.

Died: March 15, 44 B.C.E.

Roman General and Dictator

Julius Caesar is widely considered by historians to be a skilled soldier, peerless leader of men, and cunning politician. He was born into a Patrician family in Rome. As a young man Caesar served with the Roman army in Asia. He was not driven by purely military ambitions and saw generalship as an essential element in a successful Roman political career.

In 59 B.C.E. - on the heels of a successful governorship in Spain - Caesar was elected Consul and was persuaded by the two most powerful men in Rome, Pompey and Crassus, to join them in a powerful Triumvirate that dominated Roman politics at the time. In the following year he was appointed Proconsul responsible for territories that included parts of Gaul. It was an appointment that promised glory and profit, an opportunity that Caesar exploited to full effect. Rome ruled only the south of Gaul, protecting its interests through alliances with the Celtic tribes that controlled the East. These tribes were often at war with one another. With the Germanic tribes pressing from the East, it was a volatile situation that provided Caesar with the necessary pretext for incremental military interventions that in time would build up into a full-scale military campaign of conquest.

In his first year as Proconsul, Caesar defeated a migrating tribal war band from Switzerland, and crushed Germanic forces across the Rhine River. In the ensuing years Caesar extended his military operations out even wider, spanning from the Atlantic to the Rhine. In 55 and 54 B.C.E. he even sailed across the English Channel in order to conduct raids on the Celtic tribes of Britain as his personal project – there was no mandate from Rome ordering him to wage an aggressive war against Gaul.

Part of his motivation was financial. Plunder from these raids enabled him to pay off his immense debts and reward the loyalty of his legionaries. Caesar also wanted to build a reputation as an outstanding General to bolster his future claims to political power, and he wrote many first-hand accounts and memoirs of his campaigns. However, his victories were often accompanied by massacres and enslavement – Caesar would deliberately use terror to subdue resistance.

The Gauls responded finally to the mounting threat to their independence – caused by Caesar – with large-scale revolts. In the winter of 54 and 53 B.C.E. an uprising of the Belgic tribes led to desperate fighting. Caesar was then forced to confront an even larger allied military force led by the chieftain of the Averni tribe, Vercingetorix. With no real military superiority of numbers over his Gallic enemies, Caesar was required to exhibit outstanding qualities to gain victory on the field – decisive movement, willingness to take necessary risks, physical and emotional fortitude, and the ability to inspire his soldiers under constant pressure. After the siege of Alesia in 52 B.C.E., Gallic resistance was crushed.

When his extended Proconsul-ship finally ended, Caesar controlled Gaul as a celebrated Commander of loyal and battle hardened legionaries. He was finally in a strong position to claim the high political office that he desired. Back in Rome, Pompey plotted against him with the support of the Senate, who feared Caesar's growing power. Pompey was famous in his own right and was also an accomplished General and the only man in Rome to rival Caesar's reputation. When Caesar led his troops across the Rubicon River at the border with Gaul, he had full intention of attacking.

Pompey was recorded boasting that he could easily recruit enough Legions to crush the intruder, but Caesar's decisive aggression took him by surprise. Within two months, Caesar occupied all of Italy. Pompey withdrew with what remained of his army across the Adriatic to Macedonia, where he could rebuild his military forces while being protected by a large naval fleet. It was an intelligent move that forced

Caesar to take extreme risks in order to recover the momentum of his campaign of conquest.

In January 48 B.C.E. he sent part of his army across the Adriatic to Macedonia. He could not rely on reinforcing his men by sea against an enemy who maintained naval superiority. Caesar was pinned down in six months of attrition warfare outside the port. Caesar's legions were weakened by the sporadic fighting, an overall shortage of food, and spreading diseases. In July, Caesar finally succeeded in disengaging his men to march off into the northern Greece. The situation was desperate.

Instead of maintaining his previous policy of attrition warfare, however, Pompey allowed himself to be brought into a decisive and pitched battle in Thessaly, where Caesar's superior tactical skill carried him to victory. Even Pompey's death that soon followed in Egypt did not bring an end to either the Roman Civil War or Caesar's campaigning.

Caesar finally found his way to Egypt, where the Queen Cleopatra became his mistress. He gave her his full support and aided in her struggle to take the throne. He crushed Pharnaces, King of Pontus, at the battle of Zela. This was the battle that gave rise to his famous quote, "Veni, vidi, vici – I came, I saw, I conquered."

Caesar was murdered on March 15th in 44 B.C.E., by a group of Roman senators who were outraged when he declared himself dictator for life. More civil warring followed his death.

Julius Caesar vs Vercingetorix

In 52 B.C.E., Roman Proconsul Julius Caesar quashed a rebellion of tribes in Gaul led by Vercingetorix, a chieftain of the Arverni. A Roman attack on Vercingetorix's principal forces at the Hill Fort of Gergovia had ended in a sharp defeat for Caesar's army. But a subsequent attempt by Vercingetorix to harass the Romans on the march went desperately wrong. The discomfited Gauls sought safety on another unassailable hilltop at Alesia. The setback at Gergovia had taught Caesar not to risk a frontal assault again. Instead, as he himself recorded, he laid siege to Vercingetorix's army in order to starve the Gauls into submission.

Caesar's legionaries excelled in the construction of field fortifications, but the scale of the work he required of them to enclose the hill at Alesia was exceptional. About 11 miles of ditch and dirt and timber ramparts were built, modified, and strengthened. Under the General's instructions, they included devastating booby-traps such as concealed sharpened stakes. Caesar ordered a second outer line built to defend against a Gallic relief force who might launch a counterattack. This defense was even longer, at around 13 miles.

Between the lines, Caesar accumulated supplies for his forces in anticipation of his besiegers becoming the besieged. Once the Gallic relief force arrived, the battles were fought along both sides of the line and gave Caesar the chance to demonstrate his superb skills as a battlefield Commander. The General and his legionaries had been placed on the defensive, and yet Caesar's approach was positive and aggressive at all times. Every attack from Vercingetorix's men was met with a savage counterattack.

As the conflict raged, Caesar would ride to a high point within the lines so that he could survey the progress of the fighting. He would spot where trouble was developing and direct his officers to lead reserves to strengthen those units that were under the greatest pressure. At the climax of the battle on October 2, Caesar led the counterattack in person. The general gathered a force of infantry and cavalry from a quiet sector of his siege line and led these troops to the decisive point in the combat. His distinctive scarlet cloak proclaimed his presence to friend and foe alike. To coincide with his attack, Caesar ordered a second cavalry detachment to ride around the outer siege line and mount a surprise attack on the enemy's rear.

Vercingetorix at first used his cavalry to harass the Romans as they built their siege line. In early clashes with Caesar's Horsemen, the Gauls suffered significantly greater casualties. The chieftain then dispatched his mounted warriors to slip past the enemy line and ride out to their various tribes to seek help. The waiting period that followed was desperate with food and supplies dwindling rapidly, while their enemy's fortifications became ever stronger. The eventual appearance of reinforcements outside the siege line stimulated Vercingetorix to fresh efforts. He prepared his men for an assault on the Roman fortifications by making ladders and grappling hooks. But the besieged Gauls had no effective means of communicating with allied force commanders. When warriors outside the fortifications mounted a night attack, Vercingetorix's men inside the siege lines were as taken by surprise as the Romans. The Gaul's major effort came on October 2 as allied forces massed against the weakest point in the Roman defenses, a poorly sited camp. Vercingetorix dispersed his men cleverly to overstretch the defenders by pressing at many points along the inner line. But even when they penetrated the fortifications, the Gauls could not hold on to their gains. The Gauls were put to the flight, suffering heavy losses under dogged Roman pursuit. The following day, Caesar accepted Vercingetorix's surrender.

According to Plutarch, the defeated Vercingetorix emerged from Alesia on horseback, wearing his most splendid armor and with his horse richly adorned. Julius Caesar accepted the surrender of the Gauls while seated in front of his camp. He was held prisoner in Rome and paraded in chains to celebrate Caesar's triumph over the Gauls, after which he was strangled to death.

Attila the Hun
Born: 406 CE

Died: 453 CE

Emperor of the Huns

When the Asiatic nomads known as the Huns migrated into the territory along the Danube frontier of the Roman Empire, they came under the leadership of the charismatic Attila the Hun. A ferocious warrior described by his enemies as keen of judgment, Attila at first accepted tribute payments from the Romans and campaigned only in regions further east. However, the wealth of Roman lands eventually proved too tempting. From 441 – 443, Attila rampaged through the Balkans and threatened Constantinople. Four years later in 447, he switched his attention to Gaul. With this fast-moving force of Hun Horseman augmented by Ostrogoths and other Germanic tribesmen, Attila swept away all before him, laying waste to towns and cities. Only his shocking defeat at Chalons prevented Gaul from being overrun.

Attila the Hun was regularly paid tribute by rulers of many different lands, including the Roman Emperor. Attila developed a reputation for breaking peace treaties, such as when he attacked the Eastern Roman Empire. When Attila invaded the Balkans, his tribute was tripled, but when he attacked the Empire again he negotiated another treaty. When the Eastern Roman Emperor Marcian and Western Roman Emperor Valentinian the Third refused to pay tribute to Attila, he amassed a massive army of nearly 500,000 fighting men and invaded Gaul. This led to his defeat at Chalons by Aeutius, who was allied with the Visigoths.

In 452 Attila again went on the offensive and invaded northern Italy, but spared the city of Rome. Reportedly, Pope Leo I rode out to parlay with Attila and persuaded him to withdraw. But the spread of plague and famine certainly threatened to destroy the Hun Army more than any battle could. It is believed that the persuasion of Pope Leo was effective because of the rough shape of his own troops.

Attila the Hun died the following year on his wedding night after getting drunk. It is said that he choked to death in his sleep from a severe nosebleed. He left behind a divided family. Control of his empire was dispersed among his successor and other sons. Attila the Hun's lands at their peak stretched from the majority of Western Europe all the way into Asia. He left behind a terrifying reputation for savagery, adequately summed up in the title of: "Scourge of all lands".

Chapter 2: Crusaders, Castles, and Nomads

Belisarius

Born: 500

Died: 565

Byzantine General

Often recognized as the greatest of Byzantine Generals, Belisarius rose to prominence by sheer ability. He was born into a relatively obscure family in the Balkans and, as young man, served as a soldier in the Byzantine Imperial guard. Then in 527, Emperor Justinian entrusted him with his own command in the East, where the Empire faced incursions by the Persian Sassanians. Belisarius did so well that by 530 was in charge of Byzantine forces in Mesopotamia. He defeated a larger Sassanian army later in that year, but was beaten at Callinicum in 531 before being recalled to

Constantinople during peace negotiations. It was fortunate for Justinian that Belisarius was in the capital in 532 when rioters seized control of the city. While the Emperor cowered in his palace, Belisarius led his elite troops into the streets and subdued the rebellion through a ruthless massacre – as many as 30,000 citizens may have been slaughtered in the melee.

Belisarius was by then the obvious choice to spearhead Justinian's most treasured project, the reestablishment of control over what had been the Western Roman Empire, now in the hands of barbarians. Belisarius landed in North Africa and in 533 defeated the Vandals at the battle of Ad Decimum and Tricamerum before finally taking Carthage itself. In 535 it was the turn of Italy, ruled by the Ostrogoths. First taking Sicily, Belisarius moved north to seize Naples and then Rome. But throughout these campaigns, he had too few troops to occupy and control the territories gained. The Ostrogoth King finally surrendered in 540. He may have done so after Belisarius promised to declare himself Emperor of the reformed Western Roman Empire, with the Ostrogoths to be part of the Imperial forces. Their surrender delivered their impregnable capital, Ravenna, to the Byzantines, after which Belisarius reneged on his promise for reasons that remain unclear.

The reconquest did not hold, and in 544 Belisarius was back in Italy, battling a new Ostrogoth leader. By this point he had lost Justinian's favor and he withdrew into private life in 551. Belisarius emerged for one final battle in 559 when Constantinople became threatened by a marauding band of Huns. He personally led a few hundred men beyond the walls of the city and ambushed the Huns. The fight was so one sided that soon the Huns were in full retreat and left the Byzantine lands.

One legend claims that Justinian was so ungrateful for all that Belisarius had done that he had him blinded and forced to beg on the streets in his final years of life. This has never been proven, and it would seem that he spent his twilight years in comfort and dignity.

Khalid Ibn Al-Walid
Born: 592

Died: 642

Arab General

Known as the successful commander of the early period of Arab expansion, Khalid Ibn Al-Walid made an effortless transition from tribal warfare to fighting major armies. He was originally the sworn enemy of the Prophet Mohammed, but after converting to Islam, he became one of his most trusted generals. After the Prophet's death in 632, Khalid served under Caliph Abu Bakr, suppressing an Arab revolt in the Ridda Wars. He then fought in Mesopotamia, trouncing the Persian Sassanids in a lightning campaign that ended in the resounding victory at Firaz in December 633.

Ordered to the aid of Abu Bakr, who was fighting the Byzantines in Southern Syria, Khalid led his army across the Syrian desert and after more victories captured Damascus in September 634. During the siege at Damascus, Abu Bakr died and was replaced by Caliph Umar, who distrusted Khalid. Umar removed Khalid from high command, but he continued to play a leading role in Arab operations. In August 636, he achieved his greatest victory, routing a Byzantine army at the river Yarmuk. Umar finally dismissed Khalid in 638 after a religious dispute.

Charlemagne

Born: April 2, 742

Died: January 28, 814

Frankish King and Emperor

Charles the Great was the son of Pepin, the first king of the Carolingian empire. Pepin's domains at his peak of power covered most of present-day France, in addition to Belgium and areas of Germany. The single ruler of this particular extensive kingdom from 771,

Charlemagne was above all a war leader, expected to take his army on campaign every year. He is reckoned to have undertaken 30 campaigns in person in the course of his sovereignty – to maintain his authority, expand his domains, and forcibly spread the Christian faith.

Charlemagne had no standing army and no bureaucracy, however he achieved a high degree of organization and the assembly and supply of his forces. His chief nobles, the counts, were responsible for raising the various soldiers which he needed, with equipment for each and every man. The warriors brought some food with them, while extra supplies were requisitioned from landowners. The Army typically assembled in the spring season and summer and fought in the autumn. Charlemagne continuously gathered intelligence on the domain in which he intended to fight and normally prepared careful plans. He usually divided his forces in two or more columns when advancing into hostile territory, presumably mainly because a smaller sized body of men would find it easier to contend with the difficulties of movement and supply.

Charlemagne's horse cavalry were his essential troops. Retainers of the Frankish nobles, the armored horsemen were obliged to show up prepared for military service when required by the king. Armed with a lance, sword, as well as shield, they fought mounted, relying on stirrups and high-back saddle to maintain a stable seat in combat. Pitched battles were unusual, campaigns commonly comprised of skirmishes, assaults on bastioned settlements, resisting or avoiding ambushes, and much laying to waste towns and countryside. Although in the first quarter century of his sovereignty Charlemagne commanded his army in person, he was not a ruler renowned for prowess in face-to-face combat. His real qualities lay in his authority, organization, willpower, and ruthless persistence.

Charlemagne fought several wars in opposition to typically inferior resistance around his extensive borders, but even so success was certainly not assured. He faced challenging opposition from insurgents and his resources were overstretched against a variety of opponents. The campaign in which Charlemagne trampled over the Lombard kingdom of North Italy in 773 – 74 exemplified unhesitating military action. After marching across Alpine passes in columns, the Franks who emerged on the north Italian plane were too numerous for the enemy to take on. Charlemagne came to a halt at the Lombard capital, Pavia, and laid siege to the city until it capitulated. Even though further campaigns in Italy against Lombards and Byzantines were needed, a political arrangement he imposed held firm, establishing Frankish control of the northern half of Italy.

Campaigning in Iberia turned out to be more challenging. Virtually all of Spain was subjected to Muslim rule, and divisions between the Arabs and the few small Christian states that did exist gave Charlemagne an opportunity to step in. But the resulting journey in northern Spain in 778 was one of the most unfortunate disasters of his career.

At the end of an unsuccessful foray to Zaragoza, he was leading his military straight back across the Pyrenees in the rearguard when his forces were ambushed and massacred. The death of prominent Frankish nobles in this attack provided material for a well-known medieval epic: The Song of Roland. It was considered embarrassing to have fallen into this sort of trap. Later in his reign, the Franks with success occupied a protective buffer zone south of the Pyrenees, including Barcelona. Most of Charlemagne's wars were aimed across the open eastern frontier of his domains, most importantly against Saxons. These independent, pagan groups were repeatedly terrorized by Charlemagne's columns, who were always ready to rebel again when the Franks were distracted. The resistance angered Charlemagne, who is guilty of an appalling massacre of 4,500 Saxons at Verden in 782. The submission of the inspired guerrilla leader Widukind in 785 did not end the opposition, but that marked the point at which it could no longer succeed.

By the 790s Charlemagne had begun to delegate military operations to his sons or to nobles. He was not personally involved in demolishing the nomads who dominated the Danube Valley, but he did plan to construct a canal linking the Rhine and Danube to facilitate the movement of his troops – an engineering undertaking that proved to be well outside the Frank's engineering capabilities. By 800, when Charlemagne was crowned Emperor by the Pope, the age of yearly campaigns was coming to a close, as was his individual command of army operations. It established his kingdom into an empire stretching as far south of central Italy and Barcelona and as far east as the Elbe. To ensure the succession to his throne, Charlemagne crowned his son Louis the Pious as co-Emperor. When Charlemagne died the following year in 813, Louis succeeded him.

Saladin
Born: 1138

Died: March 4, 1193

Sultan of Egypt and Syria

Salah ad-Din Yusuf ibn Ayyub is the proper name for the warrior ruler familiar to Westerners as Saladin. He was a Kurd born in Tikrit in current day Iraq. His family entered the service of the Zengid ruler, Nur ad-Din, in Syria and, from 1164, Saladin accompanied his uncle on a series of military expeditions to Egypt. There he was initiated in combat, distinguishing himself in a triumph over the Egyptian Fatimids along the banks of the Nile, withstanding a lengthy siege while in the ancient city of Alexandria.

The two Kurdish warriors developed their own ambitions in Egypt, Saladin inheriting the rank his uncle had achieved as vizier at the court in 1169. Two years' time later he defeated the Caliph and seized power for himself, founding the Ayyubid dynasty. After the loss of his uncle in 1174, Saladin returned to Damascus, where he challenged the Zengids for control over Syria. The resulting struggle continued for more than a decade. While combating his fellow Muslims in Syria, Saladin initiated warfare against the Crusader Kingdoms in Palestine. Control of Jerusalem was the magnificent glittering prize he most sought. Saladin's invasion of Palestine in 1177 resulted in the successful conquest of multiple strongholds along the coastline. Underestimating the Christians and ill informed of their movements, he allowed himself to get surprised at Montgisard with his forces dispersed. The consequence was a massacre that Saladin was lucky enough to survive. He learned a lesson after the setback. For the rest of his military career he would be prudent and long-suffering, ready and waiting for a opportunity to engage his adversary on his own terms and conditions. Saladin took his revenge two years afterward in a campaign that concluded with the utter devastation of a Crusader citadel at Jacob's Ford.

It was not until 1183 that the capture of Aleppo in Syria – a crucial development in his war with the Zengids – at last freed Saladin to concentrate on defeating the Crusaders. They marched on Jerusalem, but the attack was frustrated when the Crusaders rejected battle on equal terms. No such wisdom was exercised by King Guy, a French knight who governed Jerusalem, when he encountered Saladin at Hattin in 1187. The Christian army was slaughtered in Jerusalem when confronted with an assault they could not withstand.

Saladin entered the city on October 2 1187, behaving with humanity and decency toward the defeated defenders. This was Saladin's policy of chivalry, and during the following years a considerable number of Crusader strongholds surrendered when assured of good treatment. However, his decisions to let go of aristocratic prisoners enabled many to resume battle against him. In failing health, and with limited control over the diverse elements of his military, Saladin made way for the Christians to regain the initiative. King Guy, liberated after his defeat, led a siege of Acre in 1189. Saladin failed to relieve the city before Guy was joined by fresh Crusaders from Europe in 1191, turning the balance of forces against him. He could only observe as Acre fell to the Christians, and he was defeated by Richard the Lionheart's army at Arsuf and again the following year at Jaffa.

Saladin believed that his strategies were still effective enough to prevent the Crusaders from retaking Jerusalem, but he signed a peace deal with Richard. His famous gesture of sending ice to the feverish English King formed part of a diplomatic offensive to secure the Crusader King's departure in 1192. Saladin died shortly after, while he was still in possession of the Holy City.

Saladin vs Richard the Lionheart

In August 1191, Richard the Lionheart of England led a Crusader army south alongside the Palestinian coast from Acre toward Jaffa. He intended to utilize Jaffa as a base for retaking Jerusalem from the Muslims. Conscious of the dangers that heat and thirst posed to his armored knights, Richard proceeded by slow stages, stopping to allow the supply ships that supported his army offshore to keep up. The Muslim leader Saladin - who had also been camped at Acre - followed the Crusaders on higher terrain inland. He harassed them with skirmishing raids, all while looking for the right chance to launch a decisive attack.   Richard understood it was vital for his army to maintain discipline during the march. He placed a screen of foot soldiers, including crossbowmen, on the landward flank of his column to safeguard the mounted knights. He gave strict instructions that the knights were not to respond to provocation from skirmishing rival horseman.

On September 7, 1191, approaching the town of Arsuf, Richard suspected that Saladin intended to assault in force. He rearranged his column in preparation for battle, moving forward with Elite Templars and hospitallers in the van and the rear respectively. When the Muslim onslaught began, Richard's reaction was to hold a close formation, waiting for the right moment to signal a coordinated charge. This strategy demanded the knights to remain passive while arrows rained down on them, killing many of their mounts.

Finally, discipline broke and groups of Hospitallers began to break formation and charge rashly toward the opponent, engaging in close combat. Finding himself unable to prevent the Knights, Richard joined them. The Muslims fled the carnage, only to turn again and resume their harassing attacks. By plunging into the fray, Richard had wasted overall control of his army, but his individual example was an inspiration to his Knights in battle and they finally prevailed in driving off the enemy. On the final account of casualties, Richard justly enjoyed the triumph at Arsuf.

Saladin had prepared an intelligent plan to defeat the Christian Knights, despite their superior heavy armor. He would provoke them into an attack on his forces during which they would lose formation, allowing his lighter horseman to infiltrate, encircle, and progressively eradicate them. After harrying the advancement of Richard's army with skirmishing attacks alongside their march from Jaffa, Saladin's forces waited around the plain at Arsuf. This plain had been chosen by Saladin as the location for battle mainly because it provided a good open field for his cavalry, while the flanks were secured by woods and hills.

Saladin's plan was to focus on the rear of the Crusader column, sending in first his foot skirmishers – including both Numidians and Bedouin – to strike with darts and arrows. The mounted archers would follow, swarming around the Christians to provoke them into an undisciplined charge. Unlike Richard, Saladin had absolutely no intention of fighting in person, instead observing the action from an effective vantage point at the top of a nearby hill. The battle proceeded broadly as Saladin had planned, though not with the final result he had intended. The Christians did ultimately break formation and charge in an unorganized fashion, and Saladin was in a position to respond with a forceful counterattack. Further attacks and counterattacks followed, but the Christians were ultimately more effective and better armored in the close quarter fighting. Saladin did not lose control over his army. Each time he returned his horsemen to the fight, they would be driven off with heavy losses. The failed outcome of the battle was a severe blow to the Muslim Commander's reputation. The Christian success was an indecisive one however, and resulted in Saladin reverting to harassing tactics instead of engaging Richard again in open battle. Despite the fact that Richard went on to take Jaffa, he was not able to fully utilize his gains and take Jerusalem – the supreme goal of the Crusade.

Genghis Khan

Born: 1162

Died: 1227

Mongol Khan

The creator of the Mongol Empire was originally named Temujin, the son of the chieftain of one of the many nomadic tribes inhabiting what is now Mongolia. His father was murdered when he was a child and he grew up as a resourceful survivor in a hostile environment. Success in the raids and skirmishes of endemic tribal warfare made him the leader of a growing warrior band. This allowed him to form valuable alliances with tribal leaders.

By establishing his authority over his friends and beating his enemies, he extended his control over the disconnected tribes until, in 1206, he was acknowledged as ruler of the united peoples of the steppe. As leader of the steppe tribes, he adopted his famous name, which means, "Supreme Ruler".

Every Mongol tribesman was a horseman and warrior. On their small and hearty mounts, these nomadic tent dwellers sustained campaigns over thousands of miles without a supply train. Their weapon was the composite bow, which they used in disciplined maneuvers learned through the frequent hunting of wild game. The Mongol warriors were absolute in their indifference toward the suffering of their enemies.

As Genghis Khan, Temujin harnessed the power of inter-tribal war to conduct a campaign of conquest. His first target was the Tangut Empire in what is now Northwestern China. First invaded in 1209, the Tanguts were absorbed into the Mongol Empire in the last few years of Genghis's reign. Farther south were the lands of the Jin Dynasty, descendents of steppe horseman who ruled northern China. Genghis attacked them in 1211, but ended up being blocked by the defenses of the walled towns. He returned with a deadly siege train in 1214 and captured Zhongdu the next year, even though the Jin themselves were only conquered under Genghis's successors.

The Mongols then struck westward into Muslim ruled Central Asia. The shah of the Khwarezmian Empire – which stretched from Iran to Uzbekistan – had executed a Mongol ambassador, provoking an invasion that crushed the great cities of Samarkand and Bukhara. By the time Genghis died in 1227, his armies had swept as far west as the shores of the Black Sea.

His grandson Kublai Khan would later realize his dream in the conquest of the Song Chinese, as well as invasions of Japan and Vietnam. Kublai Khan was both a Mongol Khan and Chinese Emperor.

Timur
Born: April 8, 1336

Died: February 18, 1405

Conqueror

Timur was a conqueror born into a tribe of horsemen in the area of Central Asia that is the equivalent of the Present-Day Uzbekistan. When he was young, he led a band of lawless thugs and highwaymen. He was ruthless and fought in many skirmishes and regularly robbed merchants.

He later suffered an arrow wound that left him partially paralyzed on the right side of his body. Despite this, Timur rose to a position of power by using his lawless band of fighters to help ambitious Muslim rulers. He eventually came to rule Balkh and Samarkand. Timur did not have ambition to rule greater lands than this initially, but he was an opportunist. His thirst for military conquest was sparked when a rival reformed the Mongol horde.

His rival Tokhtamysh raided Persia and Timur himself launched destructive campaigns of murder and plunder, eventually destroying Shiraz and capturing Baghdad. The two warriors finally met on the field of battle and faced off at the battle of Terek River. Timur was victorious and soon set to destroying his former rival's lands, burning and looting to the extent that the Mongol Horde was utterly destroyed. Timur now had a reputation for being a conqueror, but his thirst for blood and riches was far from sated. He achieved total victory in Asia and followed this up with a series of additional campaigns that spread from Delhi to Akara in less than 10 years.

Timur's army was primarily a traditional steppe nomad force. He had many contingents of tough mounted bowmen and used them to great effect. He divided his army efficiently with each group of 10,000 divided into 1,000, which was divided into hundreds, tens, and so on. He liked to be in control of all aspects of his army and personally determined all daily operations. Throughout the course of leading his army he developed techniques for building bridges and constructing fortified camps.

He was always on the lookout for another land to invade and another people to conquer. He had a variety of ways he would gather intelligence, often making lists of future victim states. He was successful because of his warfare style. It consisted of rapid movement and slippery tactical treachery.

He also excelled in siege warfare and would hire former residents of the populations he intended to destroy to help him plan his sieges. He employed battering rams and catapults, as well as incendiary and gunpowder devices. He was also skilled at psychological warfare and would frequently play on hopes and fears of his enemies to weaken their resolve or turn them against each other. Terror was his chief means of accomplishing this.

Whenever a new opportunity presented itself, he would strike. He once invaded northern India only because he discovered that the Sultan of Delhi had recently died. He sensed an easy opportunity to seize power. He destroyed the next Sultan and demolished the city after ransacking it.

Next he turned his eyes to Egypt where another leader had recently died, leaving a young and inexperienced ruler in his place. On his way to Egypt, he rampaged through Georgia, and finally arrived in Syria. He destroyed their army and then followed his victory by leveling the city of Aleppo.

Timur continued his journey to Egypt. He also ravaged Damascus along the way. The Sultan had attempted to defend the city and was defeated and fled. The city then surrendered, but Timur looted and massacred them regardless. Instead of continuing on to the capital at Cairo, he set his sights on the Ottoman Turks. Bayezid I became his rival and the only person capable of standing up to him.

In the summer of 1402, Timur traveled deep into Anatolia, making all effort to avoid his rival's army that was marching east in an attempt to catch him. When Bayezid realized that Timur was behind him, he had to turn back instead. By the time his soldiers discovered Timur's Army, they were exhausted and thirsty. Timur controlled all sources of water on dry plain of the battlefield, forcing his rival to attack.

The battle was long and difficult and many Ottomans fled. Eventually Bayezid was captured by Timur and he later died in captivity. Timur next seized a Christian Crusader castle and then finally returned to Samarkand and died two years later without realizing his great ambition of invading and destroying China.   Timur was a warrior and a tyrant. Despite his serious physical disability that resulted from his arrow wound, he was a successful military leader. Despite being partially paralyzed on his right side, he could still ride a horse. He was capable of walking short distances on foot, but for any greater distances he needed be carried by a servant.

The most surprising aspect of his life is that the majority of his triumphs and conquests happened when he was already in his 60s. Despite his age he preferred to campaign in person and at the head of his horsemen. He suffered along with his men. There were many hardships, and across the vast expanses of Asia they experienced many different kinds of weather.

He captured previously Mongolian lands and explored throughout what is present-day Russia. Everywhere he went he would destroy and burn and pillage and murder. He possessed great mental fortitude and was highly intelligent with a tactical mind. He enjoyed playing chess and used it as a way to sharpen his mind and hone his tactics. This logical side was illogically contrasted by his use of astrologers. When their predictions contradicted his own he would ignore them. He was exceedingly cruel and took pride in cultivating this within his own soldiers.

He preferred to fight his opponents when they were at a material and psychological disadvantage. He had a highly mobile force and would exploit this to achieve a greater chance of success. He took advantage of every possible means to divide, discourage, and destroy opposing armies. His most common warrior was a mounted archer that was equipped with a composite bow, but through his conquests he acquired a diverse array of forces including Indian elephants. On multiple occasions he would pretend to flee and lead his opponents into traps. One of his favorite tactics was leading his enemy into an encirclement. His fast-moving horsemen archers would pepper his opponents with arrows while staying safely out of reach of any attempt to counter attacks. After he had weakened his opponents from a distance, his skilled warriors would close in for the kill. He would use any and all types of weapons including sabers, spears, maces, and axes. He would never risk his own life fighting in the thick of battle. He would observe the battle from a safe distance and direct his men. He was well known for his love of brutal torture.

One witness described the destruction of Damascus: "First they seized their possessions and then tortured them with whips, knives, and fire… Often red-hot irons were set on their flesh and it caused the smoke to rise with an odor of roast meat… Then he set fire to the city of Damascus [and] all its buildings… The [entirety] of so great and large a city was reduced to a mountain of ashes."

Timur was known far and wide as a monster. His men went far beyond traditional looting and pillaging. He deliberately instructed them to terrorize, torture, rape, pillage, and use anything and everything in their power to intimidate his enemies and destroy their will to resist. He would intentionally arrange graphic and frightening displays of barbarism that he knew would have powerful psychological impacts on his enemies. He frequently built pyramids of skulls outside cities he destroyed. In Damascus he incinerated the Great Mosque and the thousands of people locked inside. It is evident that he took great personal pleasure in filling his enemies with terror when he once boasted that God had "filled both horizons with fear" of him.

Edward the Black Prince

Born: June 15, 1330

Died: June 8, 1376

English Prince

Edward, Prince of Wales, was the eldest son of Edward III. In his time he was greatly feared and seen as a brutal and cunning warrior. Known as the Black Prince because of his distinctive armor, he was described by the chronicler Jean Froissart as the "flower of chivalry of all the world" and was undoubtedly an outstanding battlefield commander.

In 1346, Edward led an army at Crecy, where he fought alongside his father. He went on to replicate Edward III's tactics in that battle – dismounted troops arranged defensively – with his own army at Poitiers 10 years later. There Edward achieved an even greater victory. The reputation he earned at Poitiers was confirmed when he defeated the Castilians and French in a pitched battle at Najera in Spain during 1367.

His battlefield style was tough and ruthless rather than glory seeking. He was well-known for his destructive rides into enemy territory, pillaging and burning on the way. He also presided over the massacre of Limoges in 1370, where thousands were killed for having switched allegiance to the King of France. By then Edward had been already suffering from the disease that would kill him before he ascended to the throne.

In the summer of 1356 Edward the Black Prince led an army from English-ruled Aquitaine through Central France, laying waste and looting French territory. At the Loire River he learned that the French King Jean II, his son the Dauphin, and the Duc d'Orleans had assembled an army and sought to bring him to battle. Edward turned back toward Aquitaine, hoping to avoid an encounter. However on September 17, outside Poitiers, a clash between English and French cavalry announced that the enemy was near. The next day, knowing that he was heavily outnumbered, Edward found a defensive position on a wooded slope, with hedges, vines, and marshy ground that could inhibit a French cavalry charge. He ordered his men to dig ditches and construct palisades.

On the morning of September 19, Edward drew up his army for battle, his knights on foot, divided into three battalions, with longbow-men in the flanks. The Prince himself took up position on high ground at the rear, with a clear view of the battleground. At his disposal he had a cavalry contingent commanded by a trusted Knight, the Captal de Buch.

The sight of the French military was daunting. Not only did it outnumber the English by two to one, but additionally consisted almost totally of armored knights, in comparison to most of the English who were lightly armed foot troops. But Edward had chosen a field that limited the numbers of troops the French could feed into battle at any one time, reducing the impact of their cavalry. The French knights were organized in three battalions on foot, one behind the other, with a cavalry spearhead of 300 men. As the French prepared to attack, Edward called upon his troops to have trust in God and obey his orders.

The initial French cavalry charge was a disaster. Funneled between the flanking archers, the French knights were brought down by arrows shot at their horses and then butchered by English men-at-arms with swords and daggers. From his vantage point the Prince saw the first French battalion come up on foot, but fell back after prolonged hand-to-hand fighting. He then saw the inexplicable flight of the second Battalion, apparently panicked by Vincent quitting the field. The third French battalion under Jean's control was still an overwhelming mass of shining armor and banners. Weary English minds wavered as the French advanced to renew combat. The archers were soon exhausted of arrows, so they threw down their bows and took out their daggers. But Edward, advised by his experienced friend Sir John Chandos, dispatched the Captal de Buch with his horsemen to circle behind the advancing French knights. Then he mounted his own charger and led his entourage into the conflict with a flourish of trumpets. Attacked simultaneously by the Captal de Buch from the backside, the French were driven back on themselves in an ever tightening circle. Amid scenes of massacre, Jean

II surrendered and was taken prisoner along with most of the surviving French nobility. The chronicler Jean Froissart wrote, "the Prince, who is courageous and harsh as a lion, took that day great pleasure."

Chapter 3: Innovators of War

The most strains were placed on military commanders in periods when changing technological or social conditions demanded rapid innovation of warfare, rendering traditional tactics obsolete. These are the time periods which most aptly represent the credo, "Adapt or die". To be successful in a time of innovation requires vision, boldness, and flexibility in the face of the enemy. Successful leaders were not afraid to adapt superior equipment and tactics to their own devices.

In China and Japan in the 16th and 17th centuries, large-scale disputes brought the powerful employment of mass armies and decisive use of gunpowder weapons. Leaders who could exploit the new style of warfare were greatly successful in conquest. The benefit gained by commanders capable of adapting new technologies effectively is a constant theme of warfare in this period. Famous examples of this include Oda Nobunaga's training of soldiers to fire arquebus in volleys – displayed at Nagashino – and Korean Admiral Yi Sun-sin's supremely effective use of large, cannon armed, armored warships against the Japanese. The crucial commanders of the period, in short, were open-minded realists who achieved superiority of force by any means available to them.

Suleiman the Magnificent
Born: November 6, 1494

Died: September 7, 1566

Ottoman Sultan

Suleiman was a Sultan of the Ottoman Empire. The Sultans of the Ottoman Turkish Empire were above all leaders who legitimized their right to rule through conquest. A young and active Sultan might expect to lead his army on campaign every year, departing from his capital in the spring and returning in winter. Theirs was a harsh life. Until the mid-16th century, the accession of a new Sultan was followed by the execution of all of his brothers. This ruthlessness was accompanied by a notable effectiveness of administration, enabling the Ottomans to support an imposing army and navy that terrorized Christian Europe in the 15th and 16th centuries. The greatest of the Ottoman Sultans, Suleiman I inherited from his father, Selim, rule of the Muslim Middle East. This included the recently conquered countries of Syria and Egypt. The new Sultan focused primarily on war with the Christian West. He took the Balkans town of Belgrade – the gateway to central Europe – in his first campaign in 1521. The next year he mounted the siege of Rhodes, the island fortress held by the formidable Knights of St. John who had previously battled his great-grandfather Mehmed the Conqueror. Suleiman's willpower and military strength finally accomplished the task, although Rhodes did not ultimately fall until midwinter. The surrender of the Knights was accepted by the Sultan in chivalrous fashion.

Having secured the Eastern Mediterranean, Suleiman concentrated on additional land campaigns in Europe. In 1526, the crushing defeat of a Hungarian army at Mohacs brought him to the border of Austria, the heart of the Christian Holy Roman Empire. Three years later he put the Empire's capital of Vienna under siege, but the city's defenses held. Facing critical supply problems as the weather worsened in the fall, Suleiman was obligated to withdraw to Constantinople. In the 1530s, the struggle with the Christian world continued and Suleiman's Admiral carried the war to Italy and the Western Mediterranean. Suleiman was then sidetracked by the challenge of Safavid of Iran, leading his military on campaigns to the east and capturing Baghdad in 1534. With the passage of time his health deteriorated. He became reclusive and had two of his sons executed for presumably plotting against him. Suleiman had long ceased personally campaigning when his forces suffered a humiliating defeat at the siege of Malta in 1565. In response to this catastrophe, the aged Sultan accompanied his army into the field for the last time. He died in his tent during the siege of Szigeth in Hungary in 1566.

Earlier in his reign, Suleiman led an army of 100,000 men to invade Hungary. On August 29, 1526, he faced a force under King Louis, in which armored knights predominated. He placed his cannon and musket equipped janissaries in an unbreakable defensive formation, screened by horsemen. As the Hungarian knights charged, Suleiman's horsemen gave way, exposing them to waiting guns while skirmishers simultaneously harassed the Knights from the flanks. During the critical moment, Suleiman ordered his cavalry forward, forcing the Hungarians to flight. Louis was killed and half of Hungary was reduced to a tributary state.

Oda Nobunaga

Born: June 23, 1534

Died: June 21, 1582

Japanese Daimyo

Oda Nobunaga is arguably the most famous, most widely fictionalized, and romanticized general in Japanese history. He was a commander of exceptional skill and political ambition. Oda Nobunaga's life did not start with the same promise he showed throughout his career. The son of the head of the Oda clan in Owari province, he earned a reputation for unruliness and this often arrogant and uncooperative nature cost him automatic succession to his father, who passed away when he was 15. Nobunaga awoke to his feeling of responsibility when his retainer, Hirade Kiyohide, committed ritual suicide (known as seppuku) in protest of his younger master's irresponsible and rash behavior. After being sobered by his sacrifice, Nobunaga forcibly wrested control of the clan from his uncle. In 1560, he launched his military career in earnest, headlining with the stunning defeat of the far larger military of rival daimyo Imagawa Yoshimoto at Okehazama, accomplishing a stunningly daring night attack on his enemy, under cover of a rainstorm.

In 1568, Nobunaga seized control of the Japanese capital Kyoto. His rising influence was opposed by rival samurai clans and by militant Buddhist sects: the warrior monks of Mount Hiei, crushed by Nobunaga in 1571, and the Ikko-ikki fundamentalist monks, reduced to subjugation in 1580. Nobunaga utilized maximum power to be successful, particularly in his victories on the Asai and Asakura clans at Anegawa in 1570, and the Takeda at Nagashino in 1575. Unsentimental about samurai values, Nobunaga allotted his peasant foot troops the leading line role, and increased the usage of the arquebus by his soldiers. It was devastatingly effective when employed by skilled infantry firing in volleys. He also made unsparing use of terror as a tool, incinerating the 20,000 inhabitants of Nagashima fortress in 1574. He promoted subordinates on merit irrespective of their origins, and so insured the effectiveness of his generals but not necessarily their commitment. At the height of his power, Nobunaga ended up being cornered by a rebellious traitor general, Akeche Mitsuhide, and committed suicide.

In the summer of 1575, Takeda Katsuyori led the army of the Takeda clan and laid siege to Nagashino, the Tokugawa clan fortress. Tokugawa Ieyasu succeeded in enlisting the aid of powerful daimyo Oda Nobunaga for a tactical gamble in defense of the fortress. Combining their forces, Nobunaga and Ieyasu advanced toward Nagashino with an Army two or three times as strong as Katsuyori's. The Takeda enjoyed a formidable military reputation, however. They had introduced the cavalry charge into Japanese warfare, performed by their mounted samurai to devastating effect against the Tokugawa at the battle of Mikatagahara in 1573. Nobunaga therefore meant to ensure that his superior numbers, which consisted mostly of peasant foot soldiers, would result in battleground success.

Nobunaga took up a protective position 165 feet behind a series of wooden stockades, an obstacle that would interrupt the momentum of the charging horsemen. The key to his battle plan was the usage of the arquebus, a matchlock musket that was present in Japanese armies since the 1540s. Until this point they had any dramatic impact in a major conflict. About 3,000 of Nobunaga's foot soldiers were equipped with these primitive firearms. He arranged them in three ranks in front of his army, but behind the protective wood stockades. They had been trained to provide concentrated fire and volleys by rank.

In the morning of June 28, Katsuyori bought his mounted samurai to attack. Followed by foot soldiers, they advanced from wooded hills down onto the plain near the stream. When the Takeda forces began crossing the stream, the signal was given for the arquebusiers to open fire. Many samurai were felled before their final headlong charge reached the stockades. Immediately upon arriving they were attacked by pike-wielding peasant foot soldiers and channeled through gaps in the fencing into killing grounds. Many others were surrounded by Oda and Tokugawa samurai with short spears and swords. Eventually, the Takeda broke and fled, pursued and hunted down by their adversaries. The battle exemplified Nobunaga's hardheaded realism. He was a commander who had no purpose for fighting without superior forces, and who had no time for the noble traditions of samurai warfare. In short, he would use any means necessary to achieve ultimate victory.

Yi Sun-sin

Born: April 28, 1545

Died: December 16, 1598

Korean Admiral

Yi Sun-sin was originally an Army Commander who earned his reputation fighting Manchu nomads on Korea's northern border. After a period out of power, he was made

Commander of the Cholla Naval District. Faced with the looming threat of a Japanese invasion, Yi took vigorous measures to prepare his fleet for war. He began collecting supplies and improving the equipment on his ships. Alongside the cannon armed warships - known as panokseon, which formed the core of his fleet - he built a number of geobukseon (turtle ships), whose upper decks were enclosed in iron plates. Yi's task as an Admiral was to maneuver these gun platforms so that his cannons - firing solid shot and incendiary rounds - destroyed the lighter Japanese warships, while avoiding being boarded by the well-armed Japanese soldiers. Yi achieved this by exploiting his superior knowledge of the sea currents and channels around the Korean coastline.

Yi is credited with 23 victories against Japan. His greatest triumph during the first invasion was the engagement at Hansando, in August 1592, where the Japanese ships had been lured into an encirclement from which only a handful escaped. Success earned him jealousy at the Korean courts, however. Yi was arrested, tortured, and relegated to common soldier. A severe naval defeat during the Second Japanese Invasion quickly brought Yi's reinstatement as Admiral.

There are many factors to consider in why Admiral Yi was so successful against the Japanese. Admiral Yi took a vested interest in his men and ensured that his soldiers, supplies, and his ships were well-maintained. He expended all efforts to replace them when necessary. The turtle ship also played a significant role in his victories. He expertly navigated them against the Japanese because he had knowledge of the Korean coast and knew the sea tides and used the terrain and weather to his advantage. Like most great leaders, he was charismatic and excelled at motivating his soldiers and sailors. He treated them with respect and dignity and in return earned their loyalty.

His turtle ships had stronger hulls than the Japanese ships of that period. They were also capable of carrying at least 20 cannons which were useful in broadsiding. He personally led development of additional types of cannons that proved useful in battle. In 1597 Admiral Yi led his ships into battle at Myeongnyang against the Japanese fleet of Toyotomi Hideyoshi. Admiral Yi brought with him at least 12 panokseon warships, and they faced off against the considerable naval force of the Japanese, which numbered 133 warships and at least 200 logistical ships.

The Japanese Navy had arrived in the Yellow Sea and sent out an advance scouting party. They soon staged a surprise attack, but were driven off. A second scouting party later launched another nighttime attack, but Yi repelled them again.

All ships were ordered to return to the Japanese Fleet when they received reports that there was Korean resistance in the area. They began to amass their fleet. Admiral Yi did not want to fight a major sea battle in such a vulnerable position, so he withdrew his forces and concealed his ships on the northern side of the strait. Positioning his ships in the strait gave him a tactical advantage. The narrow strait prevented his small group of ships from being flanked by the massive Japanese Fleet. The roughness of the currents also made it exceedingly difficult for the Japanese ships to maneuver and close in. This forced the Japanese to attack in smaller groups.

Early on the morning of October 26th, the Japanese fleet began to deploy around the bay at the end of the strait. The crews of Yi's other ships were survivors of a recent naval battle under the command of a different Admiral, and were shaken by the numerically superior Japanese fleet. It is recorded that for a time only Admiral Yi's flagship was engaged in combat. He advanced alone but soon his example of bravery drew out the other ships one by one. His warships fired both cannon and arrows and were careful to avoid Japanese boarding attempts, as this was their primary tactic of the period. Several Japanese vessels attempted to come alongside the Korean ships but were driven off or sunk with concentrated fire. The tide in the strait soon reversed. The panokseon dropped their anchors while the Japanese ships were pushed back by the tide and soon began to smash upon one another. The Japanese ships clustered and crashed, forming a target rich environment for the Korean ships. The strong tides prevented Japanese sailors from swimming safely to shore and many drowned while attempting to escape their sinking vessels. By the end of the battle, records show that nearly thirty Japanese vessels were damaged or destroyed. The defeat was crushing to the morale of the Japanese and caused difficulties in resupplying their ground forces. The victory had the opposite effect for the Korean ground forces who had previously been fighting a losing front. When word spread of Admiral Yi's victory, spirits ran high.

While this battle demonstrates the strategic prowess of Admiral Yi, this victory alone failed to slow or stop the Japanese campaign in Korea.

During the final struggle of the war at Noryang in November 1598, Yi was shot by a Japanese arquebus and died on the deck of his ship. Admiral Yi Sun-sin is considered a national hero and is celebrated by statues in a number of Korean cities, including Seoul.

Hernan Cortes
Born: 1485

Died: December 2, 1547

Spanish Conquistador

Hernan Cortes was the son of a minor Noble family and was born in the backwoods region of Castile. Seeking his fortunes in the West Indies, he sailed from Seville to Hispaniola as a colonist. He then took part in an expedition sent to Cuba where he became the Mayor of Santiago. He was later appointed to lead an expedition to the American mainland in 1518. This was his first military Command position and his ambition led him to immediately accept. To Cortes this was an opportunity to fulfill his even greater plans for power. He sailed from Cuba to Mexico with 11 ships despite having been declared a fugitive after refusing orders from Diego Velazquez, the man who gave him his mission. Cortes set off under his own initiative, planning to pursue conquest for riches and power in the interior of Mexico. Any of his crew who did not agree to participate were executed. When he finally arrived on the Mexican coast, he learned of the Aztec Empire and heard of its great riches and fortune. He defeated local natives in Tabasco and decided to bring along a native woman as his guide and translator. In order to prevent any escape and to also solidify his decision to campaign and conquest, he burned all of his ships.

Cortes devised a simple military strategy in order to conquer the Aztecs. He would march on the Aztec capital, bringing along all of his 600 men with their warhorses and cannons. He would demand that the Aztec Emperor Montezuma II accept the Christian faith and accept the Spanish monarch, Emperor Charles V, as his leader and overlord. Cortes arrogantly hoped to accomplish all this without a battle by using sheer intimidation. This was further reinforced by his belief in his own cultural superiority.

The local woman he brought along, Malinche, became his chief intelligence officer. She shared with Cortes that the Aztecs were both hated and feared by many of the other indigenous Mexican peoples. Using this information and her help, Cortes formed an alliance with the Tlaxcalans on his way to the Aztec capital of Tenochtitlan. This alliance proved vital and provided him with a large local army to reinforce his own Spaniards. The Aztec capital soon grew fearful of the strange invaders and their advance into their territory. Montezuma ordered an Aztec allied city called Cholula to provide them with hospitality, food, and rest. Once Cortes and his forces arrived inside the city however, he suspected a trap. He then ordered the mass execution of the nobility in the city. This decision put increased pressure on the Aztecs.

Cortes finally reached Tenochtitlan. Montezuma's reaction when Cortes arrived has never been explainable. There is no way to know whether Montezuma actually believed Cortes was a God. The Spaniards were arrogant upon arrival and refused to defer to the Aztecs. Montezuma invited the Spaniards into the capital, but refused entry to his native allies. Montezuma may have hoped to be able to control them, but instead he delivered himself into their hands and became Cortes's prisoner.

Cortes inherently possessed the traits of determination and self confidence. That alone was not enough, and soon greater qualities of leadership would be required of him. In the spring of 1520, a large body of Spanish soldiers were sent by Velazquez to Mexico from Cuba with the order to arrest him. Cortes marched to meet them and swiftly attacked. He overcame this larger force with a surprise attack at night. He then managed to persuade most of the men he defeated to join him, thus enlarging his army in Mexico. This was fortunate for Cortes. In the time he had been gone from the capital, an Aztec revolt had broken out. They had finally been provoked by the brutality and ruthlessness of the conquistadors. When Cortes later returned to the city, he found his men under siege. Montezuma had been killed by his own people, and this was a sign to Cortes that he needed to lead a retreat from the city.

They suffered heavy losses during the retreat. The Spanish had tried to slip away from the capital under the cover of darkness, but they were detected. They were forced to fight their way out of the city. His men were panicked by their losses, but Cortes was calm and assured his men that this was only a tactical withdrawal. He told them that they still were engaged in their conquest of the Aztec Empire.

The forces from the Aztec city continued to pursue them and soon caught up with them. The conquistadors had many advantages such as horses, steel weapons, heavy armor, crossbows, guns, cannons, and more. They were almost overwhelmed by sheer numbers, but their tactical advantages turned the tide. Cortes and five others mounted a cavalry charge with lances. The Aztec commanders were so frightened by this that they fled from the battlefield.   Cortes had managed to survive this crisis, and began to prepare for a fighting return to the capital. He sought to isolate his currently inhabited city by launching campaigns against the neighboring peoples. He demanded that they either support the Spanish or deny aid to the Aztecs. This he accomplished under threat of the sword.

Cortez imported supplies and additional troops. In time he constructed a fleet of boats to operate on the lake around Tenochtitlan. The siege lasted from May until August 1521. It consisted of a costly mixture of assaulting and retreating. Finally he captured the new Emperor and this led to an Aztec surrender on August 13. Cortes's conduct of the siege and capture was determined and thorough. Cortes returned in triumph after his victory over the Aztecs. In 1524 he led an army into Honduras and defeated the Spanish rebel Cristobal de Olid. During this journey he executed his prisoner, the former Aztec Emperor Cuauhtemoc. He then returned to Spain before traveling again to Mexico. Further attempts to organize additional conquests and explorations fail. In 1541 he arrived back in Spain and joined a disastrous expedition against pirates in Algiers. Cortes spent most of the rest of his life defending his reputation against political enemies in Spain.

Battle at Tenochtitlan

Spanish Commander Hernan Cortes meticulously prepared his forces for the siege of the Aztec capital, Tenochtitlan. It was a vast city that was built on a lake and connected to the shore by a series of causeways. One of his first actions was to cut off the city's main supply of fresh water to demoralize and deprive his enemy. To achieve control of the lake he constructed 13 Brigantines, sailing vessels large and spacious enough to carry 25 soldiers and each with a cannon mounted in the bow. Cortes took personal command of the fleet, which he then manned exclusively with Spanish troops. At the same time, Pedro de Alvarado and others were all sent to seize control of the main causeways, supported by large numbers of native allies. On June 1, the Brigantines managed to fight their way through the swarming mass of warrior-filled Aztec canoes on the lake. He soon took decisive command of the water. They were able to support troops fighting on the causeways, eventually making them impossible for the Aztecs to defend. On June 2nd, Cortes began mounting a series of coordinated attacks toward the center of the city from multiple causeways. Once in the narrow streets, the advantage of Spanish horses and cannon was lost. The Aztecs hurled missiles from the rooftops, yet the Spaniards were largely protected by their superior armor. The conquistadors had to fight their way into the city each day, for Cortes believed it was too risky to station his men in the city overnight for fear they might be cut off and surrounded.

On June 30, 69 Spanish soldiers who had been captured by the Aztecs were ritually sacrificed. This was an extremely dangerous moment for Cortez. His local allies were vital to maintaining the attack, and even his own followers depended on his maintaining an aura of invincibility and calm. He suspended the assault on the city and sent troops to intimidate the villagers in nearby settlements. This ensured there was no wave of support developing for the Aztecs. From mid-July, the daily attacks on Tenochtitlan resumed in greater force. Weakened by hunger, thirst, and the European diseases sweeping the populations, the Aztecs were far less able to defend their streets and homes, now the site of Cortes's systemic destruction and massacre. Cortez moved his headquarters on a rooftop inside the city for a better vantage point. In a letter to Emperor Charles V, he described the chaos around him and the struggles they had faced. The flight and capture of the Aztec Emperor on August 14 finally brought an end to the siege.

Gustavus Adolphus

Born: December 19, 1594

Died: November 16, 1632

King of Sweden

King Gustav II Adolf of Sweden is better known as Gustavus Adolphus. He is best remembered for his dramatic intervention in the 30 Years War, between 1630 until his death in 1632. This intervention was only the culmination of a lifetime of military struggle. Gustavus had inherited a contested throne. His Protestant father, Charles IX, usurped the crown from Sigismund, the Catholic King of Poland. As a consequence, Gustavus was at war with the Poles - with intermittent truces - throughout his reign.

Christian IV of Denmark was another enemy. A Danish army was invading Sweden when Gustavus acceded to the throne. There was bitter battling before an unfavorable peace was made with the Swedes. The agreement was reached in 1613. For Gustavus, building up his armed forces and learning how to win battles was essential to survival. However, he had inherited a decrepit Navy and a weak Army.

Gustavus was not a sailor. He had a fleet built, but the embarrassing sinking of his largest warship, the Vasa, on its maiden voyage in 1628 gave an indication of his weakness in maritime matters. His skills as a soldier were far greater. Sweden had an army of poorly trained conscript infantry and dilatory feudal cavalry, but in the first years of his reign he turned this into the best battle winning force in Europe. Gustavus learned the skills of military command firsthand. His training ground was the war against Poland in the 1620s.

He was a general who sought individual experience in every part of operations. He handled the shovel to learn about earthworks and taught himself to fire cannon to comprehend artillery. He enjoyed plunging into the thick of battle, at grave risk to his life. This bold nature earned King Gustavus the nickname of the "Lion of the North". Personal experience additionally allowed Gustavus to modify the latest tactical theories – mostly devised by the much admired Maurice of Nassau – into an effective practice of aggressive combined arms warfare. Impacted by his Polish opponents, he emphasized charging cavalry as a shock force on the battlefield.

He additionally saw his drilled, disciplined infantry as an offensive force. He would order the musketeers to fire in mass salvos to soften the enemy line before his pikemen charged. He initiated the deployment of lightweight mobile artillery within the front line. The key to this tactical concept was that the arms must support each other. The shock of firepower from cannon and musket prepared the way for the push of pike and cavalry troops.

Gustavus had this as his strategic focus in control for the Baltic. Through the 1620s, he kept out of the disputes in Germany, refusing to support the Protestant cause despite his genuine Lutheran faith. Instead, the 30 Years War came to him. Christian of Denmark was defeated in 1628, bringing the military might of the Catholic Empire – led by Wallenstein - to the Baltic coast.

This posed a direct threat to Sweden's independence. In summer 1630, Gustavus responded with a seaborne invasion of Germany, landing his army in Pomerania. The core of his force consisted of Swedish conscripts and volunteer cavalry, a much improved version of the Army he had inherited. He also recruited large numbers of mercenaries – they constituted half of his men at the start of his campaign, rising to 9/10 by its end. Swedish officers had to train these multinational professionals in Gustavus's novel tactics.

The Swedish advancement in Germany began hesitantly. Gustavus tightened his hold on Pomerania while seeking allies among the Protestant Germans. However, his failure to respond and rush to the aid of the city of Magdeburg, sacked by the Imperial Army, did nothing to help his cause. Pushing south across the Elba in summer 1631, Gustavus found a major ally in Saxony and, thus reinforced, sought battle again. Victory at Breitenfeld transformed him overnight to the most admired general in Europe.

Rather than pursuing the defeated Catholic Commander Tilly, Gustavus went on a triumphal advance through Germany and across the Rhine. At the pinnacle of his strength, Gustavus's ambitions grew. He may have thought of deposing the Hapsburg Emperor and establishing Swedish leadership of the Empire – but his army was no match for this task.

In spring 1632 - after crossing the Lech in the face of enemy forces - he eliminated Tilly at the battle of Rhine. But Wallenstein had returned to the fray and started a game of maneuver and counter maneuver in which Gustavus soon lost the strategic initiative. Forced into an attack on Wallenstein's entrenched position at the Alte Veste in August 1632, he suffered the very first defeat of his German advance.

A supply problem hit, and men started to drift away. Gustavus desperately desired to bring his opponent to battle. In November, with the rival forces shadowing one another at Lutzen, bad weather set in. Assuming that campaigning was over at the end of the year, Wallenstein began dispersing his military to winter quarters. Seeing the opportunity for an easy victory, Gustavus attacked. Wallenstein was quick to reorganize his defenses. A grim battle began, resulting in heavy losses on both sides. By the end of the day the Swedes held the field. Gustavus was dead, most likely killed after leading a cavalry charge.

Gustavus vs Tilly

Gustavus Adolphus found Tilly's Imperial troops on a low ridge, with the sun and wind behind them. There had been no opportunity for Gustavus and the Saxon Elector to coordinate the Allied armies, so they formed up separately side-by-side. The Saxons took the field on the left with the Swedish on the right.

Gustavus's infantry was organized in battalions six ranks deep. Each battalion was supported by four 3-pounder cannons. His cavalry were divided into flexible groups, stationed near his musketeers. Behind his thin front line he kept substantial reserves. Before the battle began, Gustavus spoke to his soldiers and told them to believe that God would give them victory.

An artillery duel between the two sides began. Gustavus waited for the Imperial forces to grow impatient under the bombardment and attack. He could not have anticipated that the allied Saxon army would perform poorly, driven from the field by the first enemy onslaught. As Elector John George retreated with his full army in flight, Gustavus had to continue the battle outnumbered. His left line was now open to a flanking assault.

Thanks to the good discipline and flexibility of his infantry formations, he had been ready to swiftly reposition his troops to cover the left flank. His artillery commander Torstensson directed cannon fire on the slow-moving

Imperial infantry. On the right, his cavalry and musketeers had survived a fearful battering.

Gustavus mustered his reserves and drove a body of cavalry forward in a charge that broke through to the top the ridge where Tilly was stationed. Gustavus rode unarmored to where the fighting was hardest, and urged his men forward. Pike, musket, cannon, and cavalry saber all took their toll on the weakening Imperial Army. By nightfall, Gustavus had won the battle.

Tilly led his army out of Leipzig on September 16. Previous reconnaissance had identified a suitable defensive position. Tilly was a prudent leader, and he planned to force Gustavus into an uphill frontal assault. Tilly had dense formations of pikemen, each group 1,500 strong. He hoped that his position on the hill would give him the height advantage in an artillery duel. His Second-in-Command, the aggressive Cavalry Commander Pappenheim, had no respect for Tilly's cautious strategy. Tilly ordered his cannon to start their bombardment as soon as the Swedish and Saxon forces were in range. Their cannon fire was slow and largely ineffectual at long range, failing to disrupt Gustavus's battle formations. When the Swedish cannons returned fire in the afternoon, they had considerably greater impact. Tilly still clung to his advantageous defensive position on the ridge, but Pappenheim's patience wore thin.

He launched an attack with his elite cavalry – the feared Black Cuirassiers – and swept around the Swedish right. This insubordinate attack threw Tilly into despair. He had no choice but to join the battle that had begun against the Saxons on Gustavus's left line. Once the Saxons unexpectedly retreated, Tilly found himself about to accomplish an unintended double envelopment of Gustavus's army.

Unfortunately for Tilly, Pappenheim's attacks were repulsed time after time by Gustavus's resolute horse and musket formations. Tilly then attempted to advance his densely packed columns of pikemen against the main Swedish line. This formation proved vulnerable, and his soldiers were soon devastated by Gustavus's well-managed front-line artillery. With no reserves, Tilly was helpless to respond. His attacks were repelled and his defensive position crumbled. Tilly was eventually badly wounded and carried from the field, but by that point the battle had already been lost.

Chapter 4: Monarchs and Militia

Through the late 17th century, European states with increasingly powerful centralized governments created standing armies organized into permanent regiments. Their uniformed troops were subjected to strict discipline and drill, while their officials were distinguished by clear predations of rank. Armies were also much larger than in earlier centuries – half a million troops fought at the Battle of Leipzig in 1813.

The increase in numbers was accompanied by greater firepower. The pike was soon replaced by the bayonet, allowing every foot soldier to be equipped with a firearm. The flintlock proved more reliable than previous infantry weapons and was capable of a higher rate of fire. Cannons became more mobile and efficient, with greater range and heavier weight of shot.

Commanders aspired to move formations like chess pieces to outwit and out-fight the enemy. The formal education of officers at military schools and colleges was still in its infancy – the US military Academy at West Point was established in 1802 – but of increasing significance as military theorists flourished.

Communication still had to be to be conducted in writing. The Commander had staff to assist him in this, initially in the form of personal aides. Napoleon later developed this into a sophisticated staff, as well as an organization for gathering intelligence and distributing orders. Improvements in surveying furnished generals with better maps, while accurate portable timepieces increased the accuracy of coordination between different sections of an army.

Despite these advances, Commanders generally used technology that would have been familiar to Alexander the Great. Messages still traveled by horseback and supplies were still carried slowly by cart. Intelligence depended on reconnaissance by mounted scouts and the interrogation of local people or captured enemy soldiers. Commanders often had only a vague notion of where their enemy was and knew the position of their own forces only by traveling with them. Meanwhile, the increasing size of armies multiplied the problems of logistics and control. During a campaign, much of an Army's efforts were focused on keeping their men and animals well-fed.

To a large degree, command remained direct and hands-on. Napoleon interrogated prisoners himself and surveyed the terrain in person before a battle. Commanders no longer typically led from the front, but they were likely to be a visible presence on the battlefield. They were still often exposed to enemy fire – Lord Wellington was lucky to survive Waterloo unscathed.

With the increased size of armies, battle lines sprawled over miles of terrain. The commander would select a high point to achieve the best view. But even with a spyglass, observing the entire battlefield was not feasible. In any case, his view was often obscured by smoke once the battle began. This forced him to rely still on messengers.

If it appeared that a critical engagement was taking place, a Commander might ride across the field to see what was happening. Skillful Commanders kept reserves to be utilized when necessary to reinforce a breakthrough or to block an enemy's advance. But the degree of control that may be exercised in the course of the battle was necessarily limited. Although there have been exceptions – Frederick the Great of Prussia, Charles XII of Sweden, and Britain's George II among them – it became rare for Monarchs to take personal command of his Army in the field. But Kings still liked to observe sieges and battles and sometimes overruled their commanders. Russian Emperor Alexander did this at Austerlitz in 1805 to disastrous effect. Napoleon was both Head of State and Field Commander, so he was able to make decisions without answering to anyone but himself.

Frederick the Great of Prussia planned his battles in fine detail and anticipated his Army to execute his plans like clockwork soldiers. However, the preferred leadership style of the most famous Commanders of the Napoleonic Wars – Napoleon on land and Horatio Nelson at sea – was quite different. They sought the swift and total defeat of their opponents. This was an ambition that required the abandonment of formality in favor of speed of movement and decisiveness in combat. Meticulous preparation and education remained necessary to their military success, but as a last resort they rode to victory on the wings of chaos.

Duke of Marlborough
Born: May 26, 1650

Died: June 16, 1722

English Military Commander

The future Duke of Marlborough was born John Churchill, son of an impoverished rural gentleman. Charming and handsome, he forged a position for himself at the court of Charles II through luck and lasting appeal. His sister

Arabella became the mistress of the King's Catholic brother James, Duke of York. In 1677, Churchill married Sarah Jennings, a close friend of James's daughter, Princess Anne. When James came to the throne in 1685, Churchill was soon elevated to the House of Lords.

Churchill had picked up a measure of military experience during this period and he soon proved his practical ability. Leading the King's troops, he crushed an invasion by James's nephew, the Duke of Monmouth, making a bid for the throne. But barely 3 years earlier - when William of Orange landed in England to claim the throne - Churchill shamelessly deserted James to serve the new King. William rewarded him with the title of Earl of Marlborough, yet trust was not so easily gained. In 1692 he was dismissed for a rumor of treasonous connections with James. By a stroke of good fortune, Sarah's friend Anne became Queen in 1702, the year the War of Spanish Succession began. Suddenly enjoying strong royal support, Marlborough took overall command of the Allied forces fighting

France. It was a task that would have crushed a man of lesser ability. He had to lead armies on a scale far surpassing his past experience, as well as coordinate with the Commanders and Governments of the Grand Alliance: primarily the Netherlands, Austria, and Britain itself.

They also needed to be persuaded to support his operational decisions. The cautious Dutch were obsessed with National Defense and were especially suspicious of his daring nature. It is a tribute to Marlborough's charisma that in 1704, he persuaded his allies to support a daring plan.

He intended to intervene and save the Austrian Empire from defeat by France and Bavaria. Seizing the strategic initiative, Marlborough marched his primary forces from Cologne to the Danube River, a movement conducted with excellent efficiency. It stripped the defenses of the Netherlands, for he rightly gambled that the French would follow him southward.

Finding a kindred spirit in Austria's Prince Eugene of Savoy, Marlborough inflicted a crushing defeat on the Franco-Bavarian army at Blenheim. In contrast to the sensible sieges and fortified lines favored by most of his contemporaries, Marlborough was constantly seeking the opportunity to bring his enemy to open battle. In May 1706, he led an Anglo-Dutch Army against the French at Ramillies. The opposing forces were roughly equal in number, and the French had an apparently solid defensive position.

Marlborough was often found in the thickest of the fighting, and was even unhorsed in a cavalry melee. Despite this, he succeeded in carrying the day by utilizing his tactical genius. He tricked the French Marshall Villeroi into reinforcing his left-wing, while covertly shifting his own men to the center. This massed his strength where the enemy was weakest, leading to a breakthrough. The crushing French defeat was then followed in the autumn by capturing a series of fortresses. Marlborough's last major success was at Oudenarde in July 1708. At Malplaquet the following year, the Grand Alliance achieved a Pyrrhic Victory. The French inflicted some 25,000 casualties on the Allied Army before conceding the field.

The war was proving itself costly for Marlborough in every sense. His spouse's hold on the Queen was waning, his political enemies in London were on the rise, and the Grand Alliance was wavering. He proved he was still a skilled general in 1711 when he brilliantly maneuvered the French out of their supposedly impregnable defensive lines. He achieved this with a mix of deception and a surprise night attack. But when peace was eventually sought, his political fall became inevitable. He was dismissed from command and accused in Parliament of illegal war-profiteering. Over a period of exile, Marlborough's reputation was restored. Despite this, he never commanded in battle again.

During the summer of 1704, the Duke of Marlborough led an army from Cologne on a 250 mile march south to attack Bavaria. The Bavarian Elector had sided with France against the Grand Alliance. The force reached the Danube River in good order and achieved a successful but costly storming of defenses at Donauworth. Afterward he rampaged around Bavaria. In the first week of August, a French army Commanded by Marshall Tallard arrived to support the Elector's forces. Marlborough was joined by the Austrian Army of Prince Eugene of Savoy, a Commander who shared his intrepid spirit. The two men agreed to pursue and engage the Franco-Bavarian forces.

On August 12, Marlborough and Eugene advanced along the north bank of the Danube and found the location of the enemy. From their vantage point in the church tower in the village of Tapfheim, they noticed the French and Bavarian armies in the distance. Their opponents were drawn up in a defensive position between the forest and the Nebel, a tributary of the Danube.

Some Commanders might not have chosen to take the offensive against such opposition with inferior numbers. For the Duke and Prince, however, the decision to attack was made without hesitation. Eugene was assigned to distract the Bavarians on the left of the enemy line, while Marlborough smashed the French in their center and right. The Duke noticed that the French had been too far back from the Nebel to defend properly. He gave orders for his infantry to cross the stream and hold the other bank. They would soon be joined by his cavalry, and he was confident that they would sweep away the opposing French horsemen. His infantry on the left were sent to attack the village of Blenheim.

The French were ignorant of their enemy's location, strength, and goals. They woke on August 13 to the unexpected sight of Marlborough's infantry columns marching across the plain toward them. There was a delay while Eugene's experienced troops moved on the far right, during which Marlborough's soldiers had to remain under cannon fire.

Then the message came that Eugene was ready to launch the attack. The plan went into action, probably unfolding as conceived. Marlborough's infantry then forded the Nebel river. Their devastating firepower halted all French counter-charges. The French permitted their foot troops to be pulled into a desperate protection of Blenheim village. This left their cavalry exposed without infantry support when Marlborough's horse charged them on the plain.

Eugene kept up constant military pressure on the enemy left, which remained pinned for the remainder of the battle. The Duke rode across the field throughout the entirety of the clash. He dispatched messengers and sometimes personally gave orders. At important moments he intervened. He was on hand to call up reserves from Eugene's forces when his own Dutch infantry almost gave in to a French cavalry counterattack. After a full day's combat, Tallard ended up being captured and pleaded with Marlborough for terms, but the Duke insisted on complete and unconditional surrender. Pinned against the river, the end result was that virtually the entire French center and right were killed either fighting or fleeing, or were taken prisoner.

George Washington
Born: February 22, 1732

Died: December 14, 1799

American Commander-in-Chief and President

George Washington was the first President of the United States and the Commander-in-Chief of the Continental Army during the American Revolutionary War. He is considered to be one of the Founding Fathers of the United States. George Washington made his mark on American history with his very first entry into combat. On May 28, 1754, as a new Lieutenant Colonel into the Virginia militia, he clashed with French troops in the backwoods of the Ohio Valley, firing the first shots of what became the French and Indian War. Returning to the Ohio countryside in July 1755, he brought aid to the British General Edward Braddock. He set himself apart through his calm and courageous conduct amid the mayhem that led to the victory at Monongahela. When the war ended in 1758, he married and settled down as a Virginia landowner. The American Revolution tore him from this peaceful life, however. He was elected as a Virginia delegate to the rebel Congress, and his knowledge of command within the French and Indian war made him an obvious choice to lead the Continental Army.

Washington was a conservative man, who believed in hierarchy and order. Although aware of the value of regular troops in the American wilderness, he set out to develop for the Continental Army a European-style force built around disciplined, well-trained infantry. This was a struggle to accomplish with a ragtag group of militiamen, a lack of rifles, and the quality of recruits that he had to work with. The colonies could never provide enough manpower for his needs, nor adequate money to pay for and supply such troops as there were. Washington also had to handle political machinations in Congress and stave off ambitious opponents who wished to replace him.

In the Army, Washington imposed control with necessary severity. Despite this, he always showed proper concern for the welfare of his soldiers. This method carried him through the worst of crises, from near starvation in the wintertime encampment at Valley Forge in 1777 to 78 to widespread mutinies in very early 1781. Washington realized the key to keeping his army going was this important fact – the British needed to win the war; he merely was required to not lose it.

He utilized tactics and other stratagems suitable to substandard or smaller forces. He actively avoided pitched battle where it was possible. His famous victory over British Hessian mercenaries at Trenton over Christmas 1776 ended up being, in effect, a devastatingly effective guerrilla raid. But political considerations often obliged him to stand and fight when his better judgment knew it was unwise to do so. In August 1776, he had been forced to defend New York City, leading to a defeat on Long Island from which he extricated his surviving troops with consummate skill.

In September 1777, it had been Philadelphia's turn to be defended from a British offensive. The ensuing defeat at Brandywine gave him another unsought and unfortunate chance to show how well he could manage a fighting army in retreat. He had been unable to interrupt the British withdrawal to the coast at the Battle of Monmouth in June 1778, which caused a violent argument between the usually even-tempered Washington and his subordinate, Charles Lee. After this, the Commander-in-Chief endeavored only to exercise patience while together with his army in the north. Soon the South became the main active Theater of War.

The arrival of the French Expeditionary Force in 1780 shifted the stability of the conflict back into his favor. The French Commander Rochambeau decided to place his army at Washington's disposal. They planned to trap the British forces under Lord Cornwallis at

Yorktown. Leading the British to anticipate an attack on New York City, Washington marched an Army 450 miles south to Virginia. There he forced the surprised Cornwallis to surrender. Washington took off his uniform as soon as duty allowed, having once said that the post of Commander-in-Chief was one he had utilized every effort in his power to avoid taking. George Washington would be forever remembered as a reluctant hero whose wartime leadership ushered in a new era for the American peoples.

Napoleon Bonaparte

Born: August 15, 1769

Died: May 5, 1821

French General and Emperor

Napoleon Bonaparte was a giant among men. Despite his humble beginnings, he had a keen mind and was destined for greater things. Born into an impoverished Corsican family of noble descent, Napoleon Bonaparte was commissioned as an officer in the French artillery in 1785. He escaped with his household to France at the height of the revolution in 1793. Proving himself to be a capable military officer, he achieved rapid promotion. In 1794, he survived the downfall of the ruling Jacobin family, with whom he had been closely linked.

In 1796 he married Josephine de Beauharnais, who was well connected to the Directorate – the French governing body that succeeded the Jacobins. Napoleon was the age of twenty-six when he first took command in the field. The French Army in Italy was a semi-mutinous body of men short of equipment, meals, and pay. Comprehending his soldiers mixture of crumbling self-pity, collective pride, and base aggression, he won their support with the promise of victory and plunder. He also had exceptional luck, for his very early victories could potentially have ended in disaster.

Fearing the political ambitions of a successful General, the Directorate was relieved when Napoleon's search for glory took him to Egypt. Those victories against the Egyptian

Mamelukes and Ottoman Turks were negated by Nelson's destruction of the French fleet at Aboukir Bay in 1798. Despite this, the Middle East journey provided an exotic boost toward the evolving Napoleonic legend.

Slipping back into France in 1799, Napoleon ratified his claim to power with a crushing victory over the Austrians at Marengo in 1800, and he took control over the French Nation. From that point on, Napoleon had the advantage of being both ruler and Supreme Commander of France. He could now transform the French forces with the tools necessary to fulfill his substantial military aspirations. Napoleon's defeat of Austria, Prussia, and Russia as well as campaigns between 1805 and 1809 ensured his reputation. He was soon known as one of the greatest armed forces Commanders of them all.

The basis for his victories was the rapid maneuver of large bodies of troops living off the land. Napoleon used speed of movement to accomplish a superiority of power. He preferred to determine the weakest point in an enemy line and attack there first. His army appeared unexpectedly behind the enemy or struck at enemy points in quick succession, before they could concentrate in daunting numbers. On the battleground, Napoleon wanted to throw the enemy off balance by drawing the fighting to one wing. Then he would force through with the maximum force of artillery, heavy cavalry, and infantry columns at the point where the adversary's line had weakened. Napoleon strove to impose a continent-wide boycott of British imports and this led to widening war.

The placing of his family members or marshals on European thrones aroused resentment and, in Spain, a full-scale revolt. His wedding to Josephine was annulled in 1810 and he married into the Austrian royal household, but he never achieved acceptance Europe-wide as a legitimate ruler. His campaigns became progressively costly – French casualties were around 8,000 at Austerlitz in 1805, but almost 40,000 at Wagram four years later.   Troop losses in the Russian invasion in 1812 may have already been over half a million. As the war dragged on, a megalomaniac streak began to undermine Napoleon's thinking, and his health deteriorated because of his constant campaigning. The brilliance of his battlefield tactics waned; at Borodino in 1812, he merely flung his soldiers ahead in a frontal assault against Russian defensive positions. Ultimately he attained nothing more than a Pyrrhic victory at crippling cost. Yet, he never lost his influence over his troops. He understood that citizen soldiers required heroic leadership, and that is the reason which led him to tirelessly cultivate his personal image and mythology. His skills in the large-scale defensive campaigns of 1813 to 1814 have been much admired. His capability to stage a comeback in 1815, one year after abdication, with Frenchmen flocking to serve him, says volumes for his undimmed charisma. However, from defeat at Waterloo there was no return for Napoleon.

Napoleon inspired an impressive degree of personal commitment from his soldiers. This was partly achieved through showmanship. He created the impression that he knew his men personally, taking care to greet some veterans by name as he rode up and down the lines. He also made the soldiers feel that he shared their hardships on campaign and faced the same dangers in battle, even when this was just partially true. But Napoleon's charisma is not entirely open to rational explanation. Napoleon soldiers stayed loyal to the bitter-end, no matter the odds stacked against them.

On one occasion he disguised himself and intended to visit all of his encampment's watch posts on foot. He had not taken many steps before he was recognized. It would be impossible to depict the pride swelling within the soldiers upon seeing him. Lighted straw was put in an instant upon the tops of a large number of poles, and 80,000 men appeared before the Emperor, saluting him with acclamation and adoration.

Europe had many good Generals, but they tended to focus on many things all at once. Napoleon focused his full attention on one thing, specifically the enemy's main body of forces. He would always attempt to crush it first, confident that secondary issues would then settle by themselves. Napoleon's approach to strategy disregarded the occupation of territory or fortresses. His goal was, by rapid maneuver, to bring the enemy's forces to battle at a disadvantage and destroy them. His armed forces marched separately, making fast progress living off the land, and then joined up to fight. Napoleon's specialties included maneuvering across the enemy's flank to take up a situation just to the rear. This would force his enemy to give battle. He also might adopt a central position from which to strike at various enemy armies, delivering a set of blows to defeat them one by one. On the battlefield, his victories depended on the shock effect of artillery, infantry columns, and hefty cavalry. In his early battles, surgical strikes were subtly delivered against weak points opened up in the enemy position; later, they degenerated into bludgeoning frontal assaults.

Napoleon's career was mainly a triumphal progress until around 1808. He had defeated all the major land powers in Europe. However he was unable to produce a steady new ordered government to sustain a peaceful domination of the continent. He could accomplish this neither by placing his relatives and marshals on thrones, nor by allying himself by relationship to Austrian royalty. The revolt against the French in Spain in 1808 was the beginning of waves of opposition that eventually saw Napoleon battling simultaneously against Russia, Prussia, Austria, Sweden, Britain, Spain, and Portugal. Traditional ruling classes had the ability to mobilize nationalist sentiment against France. Napoleon could no longer achieve quick victories, and in Russia and Spain attempts to have troops live off the land failed disastrously.

During Napoleon's 1805 campaign, he was drawn into a strategically perilous situation.

In October, French troops forced an Austrian army under General Mack to surrender near Ulm in Wurttemberg. However the onset of winter would find Napoleon's army at the end of extended lines of supply and communication. The forces of the Russian and Austrian allies were strengthening in Moravia, and there was a possibility that Prussia might join the anti-French coalition. Napoleon's instinct was to pursue the annihilation of his enemy's forces, despite his Marshall's arguments for a prudent withdrawal. By various stratagems, he sought to persuade his enemies that he was weak and fearful. The careful veteran Russian general Kutuzov was unmoved, favoring a waiting game. But he was soon overruled by the young and inexperienced Russian and Austrian Emperors, Alexander and Francis.

As Napoleon had intended, the Allies began preparations for an immediate offensive to crush the French military. After a careful survey of the terrain, Napoleon selected a stretch of land close to the town of Austerlitz as his battlefield, positioning his troops with clever calculation. By leaving his right-wing weak, he invited the Allies to concentrate their attack on that flank. Instead of garrisoning the Pratzen Heights, the dominant feature in the region, he left a tempting path open for the enemy to advance along. His headquarters and also the bulk of his forces were set aside on the left of his line. When the Russians and Austrians advanced to attack his right, he intended to sweep from the left, envelop, and crush them. The Allied chief of staff, General Weyrother, duly obliged Napoleon by preparing a mass assault on the French right.

Through the morning mist on December 2, Russian and Austrian columns crossed the Pratzen Heights and descended on Napoleon's right flank, which barely held its ground. At 8:30 AM Napoleon bought Soult's infantry, in the center of his formation, to move forward and occupy the supposedly deserted Pratzen Heights. Through sheer incompetence, the Allies still had a column of troops belatedly crossing the Heights, and a desperate fight developed when they collided with Soult's troops rising from the mist. Only at that point, Napoleon changed his headquarters to the Heights for a clearer view of the battle. Both sides threw in heavy cavalry and the French ended up in possession of the battlefield after much slaughter.

The main contingent of the Allied military was stalled in an attempt to break through on the French right. But Napoleon's plan for an enveloping movement from the left of his line had aborted, due to unexpected resistance by forces on the Allied right, commanded by the Russian General Bagration. As an improvised substitute for the planned left hook, Napoleon ordered Soult's man on the Pratzen to turn and attack the main body of the Allied forces from the flank and rear. The outcome was a rout. Fleeing Russian and Austrian troops suffered heavy losses. The remnants of the Russian army withdrew to continue the war, but Austrian Emperor Francis made peace on humiliating terms.

Duke of Wellington

Born: May 1, 1769

Died: September 14, 1852

British Commander

Many times in history, great conquerors find themselves matched against equally talented opponents. Lord Wellington fought Napoleon's forces at their best, and ultimately won.

The younger son from an impoverished Anglo Irish aristocratic family, Arthur Wellesley, later Duke of Wellington, entered the Army to earn a living. His first active campaign was serving within the Duke of York's disastrous journey to the Netherlands in 1794. He later said of the experience that he learned, "What not to do".

His career breakthrough owed much to the appointment of his brother as Governor General in India, which maximized his chances of advancement in wars against Indian states. But his exceptional abilities shone through for the first time in tricky disputes with the Maratha Confederacy. Wellington later judged his victory over the Marathas at Assaye in 1803 as the best thing he ever did "in the way of fighting". It was certainly one of the riskiest, for he had two horses killed under him during the battle.

Wellesley was still no more than an officer of acknowledged competence when the Napoleonic Wars took him to Portugal, invaded by France, in summer 1808. His first battle in command against the French, at Vimeiro in August, was an indication of much to come. With skillful implementation of his sturdy, disciplined infantry in line, backed by cannon firing rounds of shrapnel, he drove off the attack of the French forces while inflicting heavy losses. However, the results of this victory looked set to ruin his career. Because of the convention of Cintra, his superiors agreed to ship the defeated French back to France including their weapons and booty. In the resulting uproar in Britain, Wellesley had to defend himself as not being accountable for this extraordinary decision. He was not merely exonerated, but additionally persuaded the government to send him back to Portugal with command of the considerable army.

The Peninsular Campaign fought by Wellington – as he then became known – between 1809 in 1814 is a classic of military history. Its success was attributed to his exact assessment of the broad strategic situation. He correctly judged it would be impossible for the thinly-spread French military to concentrate adequate troops to crush his Anglo-Portuguese forces, while simultaneously coping with pressure from Spanish guerrillas and regulars. He turned Lisbon into an unassailable base where he could sit, amply supplied by sea, while the French starved in the impoverished countryside outside his fortified lines.

A harsh disciplinarian, Wellington worked his troops up into a fine fighting force. On the offensive, his marches were meticulously arranged, with the fullest consideration directed at maintaining supplies. He was cautious out of necessity, because until 1813 the French forces in the Peninsula greatly outnumbered his own. He was always ready to concede ground to keep his Army intact. But Wellington could be strong and aggressive at the right moment, as he demonstrated in his striking victory at Salamanca in July 1812. This ended up being an improvised opportunistic attack on a French Army that had been momentarily overextended, maneuvering around the British flank. With a superior Army in the Campaigns of 1813 to 1814, he kept up relentless forward momentum until the French finally surrendered. Wellington was already a national hero when he faced Napoleon in person as commander-in-chief of British and Netherlands forces in Belgium in June 1815. Victory at Waterloo would secure his place among the greatest of Generals.

The Duke of Wellington intended to fight a defensive battle, reacting to Napoleon's moves. Only the arrival of Gen. Blucher's Prussian forces would enable him to win. Concealed from Napoleon's cannon, Wellington positioned the bulk of his troops on the reverse slope of the ridge of Mont St. Jean. He then garrisoned the Chateau of Hougoumont and the farm of La Haye Sainte, directly in front of his line. Another substantial division of 18,000 troops ended up being stationed at Halle, far to the right of the battlefield, to rebuff a possible French flanking move that in this case never came.

At first, Wellington took up a vantage point by an elm tree, from where he issued a stream of scribbled orders, focusing initially on the desperate defense of Hougoumont. As the French dispatched troops forward throughout the afternoon, Wellington had limited control of events as the smoke obscured the battleground. An important charge by Scottish cavalry happened later without his orders. He rode to wherever the fighting was heaviest, observing his infantry squares and assuring his men of his presence. At times the line threatened to crumble, but he directed reserves to shore up their defenses. Wellington did not take the offensive until the late night, when the French had been broken by his troops durable resistance and persistent musket fire.

Napoleon faced the battle with two misconceptions. He underestimated the fighting spirit of Wellington's army, and he thought that the Prussians would not march to join Wellington following their defeat earlier at the battle of Ligny. Marshal Grouchy, facing the Prussian forces at Wavre with 30,000 men, was presented with confusing orders that kept him immobile as Blucher sent three Prussian Corps to attack Napoleon.

Napoleon planned to open with the diversionary attack on the stronghold of Hougoumont on Wellington's right, followed by a straightforward frontal assault on the Allied center. The method would force Wellington's Army west and Blucher's troops eastward. When Marshall Soult queried the wisdom of the tactics, Napoleon snapped that Wellington was a "bad general" and that defeating the British soldiers in battle would be nothing more difficult than eating breakfast.

The preliminary attack on Hougoumont did not go as planned. Ever-increasing numbers of French troops were drawn in during the day to attempt in vain to seize the stronghold. The frontal attack on Wellington's center was repulsed by infantry fire, as was a cavalry charge. However Napoleon was able to punish the British cavalry once they continued their charge too far. Through the afternoon, tactical control would shift from Napoleon at the Inn of La Belle Alliance to Marshal Ney on the front line. Ney led a series of costly cavalry attacks which were unaided by infantry.

Meanwhile, Napoleon had to divert forces to face the Prussians arriving to his right and rear. Ney focused on capturing La Haye Sainte. This success allowed him to move his cannons forward, and they decimated the British infantry's square formations at close range. Pressure from Blucher was mounting and Napoleon needed to finish wearing down Wellington quickly. He sent his Imperial Guard into combat. When they were sent into retreat by the Duke's infantry, Napoleon had lost the day. He failed to organize a fighting retreat and his army was ultimately routed.

Horatio Nelson

Born: September 29, 1758

Died: October 21, 1805

British Admiral

The son of a Norfolk clergyman, Horatio Nelson joined the Royal Navy as a boy. He had traveled to the West Indies, America, India, and the Arctic by the time he was 18. He had a stroke of fortune when his Uncle Maurice Suckling ended up being given control of the Navy in 1776. This key influence was combined with Nelson's inherent skill in tactics. Nelson was able to advance rapidly to the coveted rank of Post-Captain. To advance and receive promotions within the Royal Navy after this was achieved only by gaining seniority. His career up to the outbreak of war with Revolutionary France in 1793 was respectable but average. The war presented a chance for advancement and fame. Serving with the Mediterranean Fleet, Nelson's cunning and eagerness for action was soon noticed. He received favorable attention from his Commanders-in-Chief, first Lord Hood and then John Jervis. His spectacular rise to public celebrity, however, only began at the Battle of Cape St. Vincent in February 1797.

Nelson was a belated addition to Jervis's squadron of 15 Ships of the Line. They then intercepted 27 Spanish Ships of the Line off the coast of Portugal. Despite their superior numbers, the Spanish were eager to escape engagement and sail for port. Commanding the 74-gun HMS Captain and sailing close to the backside of Jervice's line of battle, Nelson broke from the formation and engaged the enemy on his own. His initiative halted the enemy retreat. Even though the Captain was poorly damaged before other British ships came to its support, Nelson succeeded in boarding and accepting the surrender of two large Spanish vessels, San Nicholas and San Jose, which had collided in the confusion. Although leaving position in the line of battle was most unusual, the initiative that Nelson had shown was actually fully in line with Royal Navy tradition and certainly approved by Jervis. But Nelson's subsequent behavior in publicizing his own role in the battle and claiming more credit than was due did not endear him to others. Self advertisement was one of several failings that began to feature as a counter-point to the heroic virtues he so amply exhibited.

Nelson's conquering of the French at the battle of the Nile at Aboukir Bay in 1798 made him the most celebrated man in Britain. It exemplified the distinctive style of his leadership and tactics. As the Commander of the Squadron, he had molded the Captains of the ships serving under him into a 'band of brothers'. In sync with their leader and fully versed in his way of fighting, they could be relied on to use their initiative in implementing his broad tactical concepts. Nelson's preference was always for attack, seeking to create a pell-mell battle – a great scrimmage in which enemy ships would lose formation and be destroyed by superior British gunnery at close range. He saw local superiority in numbers by focusing all his force on one part of the enemy line. The rest was left out of the fight, to be dealt with later on. His goal was easy: the complete destruction of the enemy fleet. He achieved this so successfully at Aboukir Bay that his reputation largely survived the subsequent scandals: his affair with Lady Hamilton and his commitment to the Royal Courtroom of Naples. That later led him to be complicit in the massacre of opponents of that repressive regime and to disobey orders to rejoin the Mediterranean Fleet. He instead returned to England by land with Lady Hamilton.

Nelson's willingness to take chances, as shown at Aboukir Bay, ended up being repeated at Copenhagen in 1801. These were operations that could potentially have gone badly awry. The same was true of his climactic battle at Trafalgar in 1805. Nelson was determined to engage and destroy the combined French and Spanish fleet that sailed out of Cadiz, despite the fact that he had inferior strength – 27 ships of the line to 33 – and knew that failure would be disastrous for Britain. Nelson planned for an attack in two squadrons. Each would approach at right angles of the Franco Spanish line, then cross it at different points. This would engage the enemy center and backside, leaving the Vanguard initially cut out of the battle. He led one squadron from HMS Victory, hoisting the English flag that called upon every man to do his duty. Nelson seemed possessed and entered the fray with a death wish, exposing himself so blatantly to fire that survival would be surprising. It was a tribute to his delegating form of leadership that the battle continued to an effective conclusion after his death. He had been deservedly accorded a magnificent State Funeral.

Standing on the quarter-deck of HMS Victory, Nelson was shot by a soldier in the rigging of the French ship Redoubtable. He was then carried below decks, where he died three hours later.

Rear Admiral Horatio Nelson, commanding a squadron of 14 ships, had been searching for the Egypt-bound French Fleet since May 1798. But Napoleon's army had eluded him and landed at Aboukir Bay in July. It had been here, on the afternoon of August 1, that Nelson discovered Napoleon's naval escort anchored in line. Although outgunned by the French ships and uncertain of the depths and channels in the sandy bay, Nelson ordered an immediate attack. Nelson's intention soon became clear: to attack the van and center of the enemy line. He had prepared to defeat them while in unfavorable winds to prevent the ships of his adversary's rear formation from joining the battle. Beyond this, he trusted his Captains to use their initiative, in accord with his preference for engaging the opponent at close quarters with unsparing aggression. He ordered his ships to display lights that would identify them as allies after nightfall. They also readied their anchors to hold them in place for broadside fire against a stationary enemy. As Nelson's Captains raced one another for the privilege of entering the Bay first, his chief concerns were to keep the squadron in reasonably tight formation and avoid ships running aground. Measurements were taken to determine the water's depth, thus determining a safe passage into the Bay.

The French Admiral, Francois-Paul Brueys, was fatally surprised by Nelson's decision to attack so late in the day. His decks were still not cleared for battle when the first British ship, Capt. Thomas Foley's Goliath, arrived. On his own initiative, Foley sailed around the French ship and anchored in the shallow waters between the port side of Brueys' line and the shore. He was then followed in this wholly unexpected and hazardous maneuver by four of his colleagues. The five 74-gun ships of the French van discovered themselves under fire from opposite sides as other British ships, including Nelson's Vanguard, sailed up to starboard. The fighting was savage, but as darkness fell the French vanguard was blasted into submission. Nelson himself was a casualty in this phase of the battle, struck on the forehead by a bullet that would leave him temporarily blinded. Analyzed by a surgeon, he was found to have only a superficial wound. Ignoring advice to remain below, he went on deck to witness the end of the battle.

In the French center, the vast 120 gun flagship L'Orient had dueled with the British 74-gun Bellerophon under Captain Henry Darby. Badly damaged, Bellerophon withdrew, but only after inflicting heavy casualties – including Brueys, blasted in half by a cannonball. The rearmost British vessels belatedly joined up with the battle, leading themselves toward the action by the gun flashes in the darkness, and attacked L'Orient. At around 10 PM the French flagship caught fire, its powder magazine then exploding. The remainder of the battle ended up being in effect a mopping up procedure. The next morning, Villeneuve, in charge of the passive French rear, slipped away with two Ships of the Line and two Frigates, the only French vessels to successfully flee the debacle.

Chapter 5: Empires and Industry

Helmut von Moltke the Elder
Born: October 26, 1800

Died: April 24, 1891

Prussian Chief of General Staff

Understood as the Elder to distinguish him from his nephew, a World War I Commander. Helmuth von Moltke ended up being the architect of Prussian military supremacy in mid-19th century Europe. The son of an impoverished aristocratic Army Officer, he had been brought up in Denmark. Particularly different from the traditional, boorish type of Prussian officer, Moltke was an intellectual with quiet manners and considerable literary talent. He progressed within the Prussian army because Prussia had recognized the requirement for intelligent and professionally capable Staff Officers, and because his cultured manner made him an eligible bachelor, attracting the favor of the royal family. During the first four decades of Moltke's career, Prussia was at peace and his only firsthand experience in combat occurred in 1839 when he was sent to serve the Ottoman Empire, and he commanded the Turkish artillery in a battle against Egypt.

As chief of the Prussian General Staff in 1857, Moltke revealed impressive energy and drive through radical involvement in organization, planning, and training. However, his personal status, and that of the General Staff, was at first very uncertain. In 1864, when Prussia went to war with Denmark, Command ended up being entrusted to an 80-year-old General who ignored Moltke's procedure for the conduct of operations. When Moltke was allowed to take control, he brought the war to a swift, successful conclusion. In the process he won the confidence of King Wilhelm I. In 1866, when a major war broke out with Austria, Moltke was free to act as the Commander-in-Chief, using royal decree to issue orders to Army and Divisional Commanders who outranked him in terms of formal social and military hierarchy. Despite his success, some Officers still resented receiving instructions from a man who they regarded as an obscure military bureaucrat.

The rapid defeat of Austria made Moltke a celebrity, and left his authority unquestionable. The war showed his ability to combine prepared planning with a keen appreciation of the chaotic reality of conflict. The key to precious triumph lay within the efficient mobilization of almost 300,000 men and their gear by railway and trains. This was in line with precise timetables drawn up because of the railroad section of the General Staff. This enabled Moltke to seize the initiative from the outset.

Moltke planned for the three armies to maneuver separately, then come together to destroy the Austrian forces in a decisive battle. He understood the need for flexibility and did not attempt to control the campaign at length. His crisp, clear written instructions – early on in the war sent by telegram from Berlin – always allowed commanders a measure of freedom to exercise their own initiative. Likewise, he relied upon the inner circle of his General Staff to make independent judgments in accordance with his strategy.

The climactic struggle of Koniggratz on July 3, 1866 was almost a tragedy, when the last of Moltke's three armies failed to arrive until halfway through the day. Triumph was finally achieved with their aid, after which Austria sued for peace. When Prussia went to war with France in 1870, Moltke ensured that his Army was the best-trained in Europe, and that its officers and NCOs were imbued with a shared ethos and tactical doctrine. France's mobilization was a shambles, while Prussian mobilization was faultless. Overcoming temporary confusion and errors as his armies advanced into eastern France, Moltke issued continuously altering orders to meet the quickly developing situation.

By remaining versatile, Moltke was able to lure the courageous but disorganized French field armies into traps at both Metz and Sedan, from which they would not escape. With the surrender of Paris after an extended siege in January 1871, Moltke was recognized as the architect of a military victory that soon made a Prussian-led Germany the dominant power in Europe. The battle at Koniggratz led to 44,000 Austrian casualties, compared with only 9,000 on the Prussian side.

The Battle of Sedan

Moltke and his staff traveled with the Royal Headquarters of the Prussian King, Wilhelm I. They kept up with the movements of the 3rd Army under Crown Prince Friedrich Wilhelm of Prussia, as well as the Army of the Meuse under Crown Prince Albert of Saxony. Both Crown Princes acted upon Moltke's orders, although he permitted them broad scope to decide just how these orders were carried out. Moltke was unclear of the intentions of the French. At first, he assumed that MacMahon would fall back toward Paris, and in response prepared to march westward. On August 25, after studying reports in French newspapers and with proof provided from his own cavalry patrols, Moltke decided that MacMahon must have embarked upon a march northeast to join up with Bazaine. Recognizing an unmissable opportunity for a decisive victory, he ordered his armies to travel northward. Using his men assertively to keep in range with the enemy, he was able to catch up with MacMahon, who was crossing the Meuse River near Sedan on August 30.

The following day, Moltke believed that the French would attempt to escape. In order to prevent this, Moltke sent fresh troops across the river both east and west of the French Army – the path northward was blocked by the Belgian border. As the French remained passively inside Sedan, Moltke caught them in a trap.

At dawn on September 1st, Moltke's armies, outnumbering the French with 200,000 men to 120,000 men, were in place to attack. By early afternoon they had completed the encirclement of Sedan and begin assaulting the

French defenses. Although the battle was intense and casualties high, Moltke had no doubt that the end result would be victory. Watching proceedings from a hilltop alongside King Wilhelm, Bismarck, and other dignitaries, Moltke did not issue a single written order that entire day until the battle was over, leaving his Army and Corps Commanders to do their jobs and force the French to surrender.

MacMahon's dilemma was whether to try to link up with Bazaine's army or to fall back toward Paris. The French Emperor, Napoleon III, who had joined MacMahon at Chalons, urged withdrawal westward. But MacMahon had chosen a long march around the Prussian flank to meet Bazaine, who he optimistically assumed to be breaking out of Metz. MacMahon's army was not prepared to execute a maneuver on such a grand scale – they had no maps of the terrain, previously having assumed to be battling in Germany. Slowed by logistical difficulties, they were additionally confused by their Commander's hesitation.

On the evening of August 27, MacMahon issued orders to turn toward Paris, and then cancelled this command the next early morning. Inexplicably failing to send his cavalry patrol in the direction of the Prussian armies, MacMahon ended up being ignorant of their strength and their position. The unexpected clash with the Prussians on August 30 resulting in the French being forced to complete the hasty, panic stricken crossing of the Meuse. To rest and regroup his weary forces, MacMahon allowed them to stay in Sedan, the fortress town where much-needed food and ammunition were to be found. He could still have made a fighting escape to the West on August 31, but did nothing, while Moltke's armies crossed the Meuse unopposed. MacMahon designated September 1 as a rest day, but at 4 AM the Prussians launched an attack. MacMahon was wounded early on by an artillery shell. In a debacle typical of the confusion in the French camp, he was forced first by General Auguste Ducrot, and then by General Emmanuel de Wimpffen, to get authorization from the government in Paris. It made no difference who gave the orders, because French military doctrine ultimately determined that there would be no retreat. Prussian artillery dominated the battlefield. Attempts to break out by cavalry and infantry showed immense bravery but could not succeed. Napoleon III humanely insisted on a surrender to save lives. More than 100,000 French soldiers were taken prisoner.

The American Civil War

Many of the finest serving US Army Officers decided to support the Confederacy in the beginning of the War. Men like Robert E. Lee and Jeb Stuart brought professionalism and flair to high command that the Union Generals initially could not match. Yet the Confederate Commanders labored at all times under a severe deficiency of manpower and material. Whereas many Commanders - such as Joseph Johnston - demanded caution to conserve forces, others, including Lee and Stonewall Jackson, believed that only achieving offensive victories could give the Confederates a chance, since they were fighting against the odds.

Stonewall Jackson
Born: January 21, 1824

Died: May 10, 1863

Confederate General

Born in Clarksburg, Virginia, Thomas Jackson was orphaned at the age of six and grew up clumsy, introverted, eccentric, and prone to psychosomatic illnesses. He did not shine at West Point, but after graduating in 1846, proved his worth as a fighting officer in the Mexican war. In 1851, he quit the Army to attend Virginia Military Institute, and at the same time he became a devout Calvinist, and he believed his life was directed by divine predestination. The Institute cadets unkindly dubbed him "Fool Tom".

Jackson entered the Civil War with his home state in April 1861, and his evident professionalism saw him promoted in just two months from Colonel to Brigadier General. Leading a Virginia Brigade at the first Bull Run on July 21, his infantry stood firm against the Union onslaught. Confederate General Barnard E. Bee cried, "There stands Jackson like a stone wall!"

Although it is perhaps not certain this was meant as a compliment, Jackson ended up being known as Stonewall ever after. Jackson's reputation as a brilliant General was attained in the Shenandoah Valley campaign of spring 1862. Outnumbered four to one, his small force of soldiers taunted and stood up to the Union Army.

Unforgiving of weakness and a harsh disciplinarian, Jackson was a tough man to serve under. But by driving his troops pitilessly on forced marches, he ran circles around the enemy and continuously brought them to fight at times of his own choosing. Sheer fatigue may account for Jackson's uncharacteristically lethargic performance under Robert E. Lee in the Seven

Day's Battles in June 1862. This did not prevent him from becoming Lee's most trusted colleague.

In August, his seizure of Manassas Rail Junction by a hard driven flanking march resulted in a Confederate victory at the Second Battle of Bull Run. He fought alongside Lee in the desperate defensive battle at Antietam in September, and again at the crushing repulse of the Union attacks at Fredericksburg in December. Chancellorsville in May 1863 was both Jackson's victory and his downfall. Wounded by friendly fire from one of his own infantryman, he died of complications after surgery. Lee suffered his loss deeply and it was a severe setback for the Confederacy. Jackson in life had the assurance of a man convinced his actions were fulfilling God's plan for the world. He sought to mystify, mislead, and surprise the enemy to make up for the heavy odds against the Confederates.

Chancellorsville

From his headquarters at Chancellorsville Mansion, Union General Joseph Hooker, with 130,000 men to Robert E. Lee's 60,000 men, launched an offensive against the Confederates. Learning that Hooker's right flank was exposed, Lee sent Jackson on a circuitous 12 mile march to attack it, while he himself engaged the Union Army frontally at Chancellorsville. Jackson's maneuver did not go unnoticed, and was taken by most of the Union Commanders as a sign of retreat. When Jackson burst out on Hooker's right flank on May 2, his assault was devastating and the Union Corps was routed.

Fighting continued into the evening, within the course of which Jackson was shot in the arm by one of his own pickets. Command of the Corps fell to Jeb Stuart. With Lee hammering his east flank, Hooker was at last obligated to withdraw, leaving Lee victorious. But when he heard that Jackson's arm had been amputated, he commented that, "He has lost his left arm, but I have lost my right." His words were prophetic, for Jackson died of pneumonia on May 10.

Robert E. Lee

Born: January 19, 1807

Died: October 12, 1870

Confederate General

Robert E. Lee, the quintessential Virginia gentleman, was the son of the American Revolutionary War hero and former Governor Major General Henry Lee. Second in his class at West Point, he entered the elite corps of engineers and invested almost 2 years supervising both civil and military engineering projects. His evident ability earned him a place on General Winfield Scott's staff for the invasion of Mexico in 1847. Entrusted with reconnaissance missions, he twice led troops on routes yet discovered around the flanks of Mexican forces, thereby contributing to American victories at Sierro Gordo and Churubusco.

These excitements were soon over, though, as Lee returned to a quiet career within the peacetime Army. By the late 1850s, Lee was a

Lieutenant-Colonel commanding cavalry in Texas. By chance, he had gone back to Virginia in 1859 when anti-slavery activists led by John Brown attacked the US arsenal at Harper's Ferry. Lee was ordered to the scene and directed the assault that led to the capture of Brown. The Harper's Ferry raid was a sign of increasing division on the slavery issue. Although Lee owned slaves himself, he considered slavery a bad thing. He didn't want the breakup of the Union, but was loyal first and foremost to Virginia.   Turning down an offer of Senior Command in the Union Army, in April 1861 he sided with the Confederacy. President Jefferson Davis made him a General and took him as his closest military adviser. As Lee sent men to dig fortifications in front of Richmond, President David couldn't predict that this polite professional soldier would turn out to be an aggressive Field Commander. Appointed to take the place of the wounded Joseph Johnston, Lee was responsible for the Army in the Peninsula, as well as the rapidly launched offensive known as the Seven Day's Battles.

Commanding in battle for the very first time unsurprisingly resulted in Lee making plenty of early mistakes. It was his good fortune that his adversary, George B. McClellan, ended up being so effortlessly unnerved and so willing to withdraw when attacked. Lee's other great swing of luck was discovering an ideal partner in Stonewall Jackson. Lee and Jackson had contrasting temperaments – Lee was cool and poised, Jackson driven and intense – but they shared the view that only aggressive tactics and an offensive strategy offered the South any hope against the Union's much larger, better equipped armies.

Lee was prepared face the risk of dividing his forces, and in doing so gave Jackson free rein. Jackson found success by attacking the enemy's weak points, utilizing swift and unexpected maneuvers. This was the key of their combined success at the Second Battle of Bull Run (known as the Second Battle of Manassas to the Confederates) and Chancellorsville. Their commitment to this strategic offensive soon overstretched Confederate resources.   Lee's September 1862 invasion of Maryland nearly resulted in catastrophe at Antietam, and at Gettysburg the next year. His invasion of Pennsylvania proved costly, and it was when the Union forces took the offensive that Lee and his troops performed best. At Fredericksburg in December 1862, Union troops were slaughtered in an ill-advised assault on Lee's well-prepared defensive position. This combined with his subsequent triumph at Chancellorsville was a decisive counter-punch against advancing Union army. Lee's plan was brilliant in conception and execution.

The loss of Jackson in the aftermath of Chancellorsville was a serious blow to Lee. He had no other subordinate with an independent capacity for aggressive maneuvers. With the absence of Jackson, he saw no alternative at Gettysburg but the frontal assaults that culminated in the infamous Pickett's Charge, repulsed with grievous losses. For the rest of the war, the Confederates had been forced on the defensive. Lee offered to resign, but no one could be found to take his place. Facing Ulysses S. Grant in 1864, Lee fought a skillful series of protective actions and imposed hefty casualties on advancing Union forces that outnumbered his troops by two to one. His dwindling army was then pinned down in St. Petersburg – it had been absolute loyalty to Lee as their leader, and he felt firm in this fact. Eventually cornered at Appomattox, Lee opted for a dignified surrender.

Created out of nothing in the beginning for the Civil War, the Confederate Army was initially a volunteer force, with conscription introduced in 1862. It had been an all white army – only at the very end was any attempt made to enlist black slaves. The Confederate troops, convinced that they were fighting in defense of their homes and families, on average showed greater commitment than the Union soldiers. Often underfed and short of every necessity of war, they fought with a significant courage that Lee said, "entitles them to rank with the soldiers of any army and at any time". Out of a total of nearly one million men who served in the Confederate forces, one fourth died in combat or as a result of disease.

Sharpsburg

On September 15, motivated by the news that Jackson had taken Harper's Ferry, Lee decided to stand and fight at Sharpsburg. Ordering Jackson's men along with other scattered forces to join him, he established the defensive line exploiting existing features – hills, fences, and the sunken road. His strength increased as more forces flocked to him. Lee then finally encountered McClellan across Antietam Creek. Skirmishes on the evening of September 16 revealed Union soldiers across the creek had been assembling on Lee's left. The next morning he was well prepared to face an onslaught from any direction. As the battle unfolded, Lee stayed in close contact with the fighting, shifting soldiers quickly to places where collapse threatened. Divisions had been forced into the desperate struggle in the cornfield.

Lee's aggressive use of artillery compensated for his inferior numbers of infantry, but he was greatly relieved when the final Division from Harper's Ferry under A.P. Hill was sighted marching toward the battlefield. His arrival in mid afternoon saved Lee's right flank from being overrun, forcing Union troops back into the creek. Holding his position the following day, Lee was then allowed to stage a nighttime withdrawal unmolested across the Potomac.

September 15, President Lincoln wired McClellan: "Destroy the rebel army, if possible." It seemed possible, for he had some 75,000 soldiers, twice Lee's strength, and the Union troops were well-equipped and in excellent morale. McClellan devised a neat plan to break Lee. Three Corps would strike the Confederate left in overwhelming force, while Ambrose Burnside's Corps on the other flank would cut off

Lee's only line of retreat. Two Corps had been held in reserve, along with all McClellan's cavalry. The cavalry would then mount a final annihilating attack on the trapped and weakened enemy. The execution of this plan on September 17 was thwarted by two factors. One was McClellan's distance from the battle: he established his headquarters at house about a mile from the fighting and never left. This meant he could not successfully coordinate his Corps Commanders, who made their assault sequentially. By the time Burnside was ordered to try crossing Antietam Creek, the fighting from the Confederate left had subsided. McClellan also grossly overestimated Lee's forces and held onto his reserves rather than commit them to the battle. When the bravery of Union infantry at last overcame stubborn resistance at the sunken road, the Confederate center was exposed. But McClellan refused a request from the Reserve Corps Commander to attack. Because of this, 20,000 Union soldiers never fired a shot.

McClellan was especially criticized for his failure to renew the battle on September 18. Both sides had sustained heavy losses: 12,000 Union casualties to 10,000 Confederate made it the costliest day's fighting in US history. McClellan's unused reserves alone were nearly equal in number to Lee's remaining healthy troops, however the Confederates were allowed to get away. While it may be questionable who won the battle, it is clear who showed better Generalship: Lincoln fired McClellan three weeks later.

Ulysses S. Grant
Born: April 27, 1822

Died: July 23, 1885

Union General and US President

The son of the tanner and small-town mayor in Ohio, Ulysses Grant entered the US military Academy at West Point wishing to be safe for life – that is, ensured a career and an income. By mistake, he ended up being assigned the middle initial S, which he held for life. He

distinguished himself only in horsemanship –
but upon graduating, ended up being assigned to
the infantry. Serving in the Mexican War as a
Regimental Quartermaster, he saw a good deal of
action, proving he had the gift of physical
courage – a Union soldier would later say of him,
"Ulysses don't scare worth a damn". His military
talent was noticed, but this did him no good in
the subsequent years. In 1854, posted to
California far from his home, he suddenly
resigned from the Army. Rumor said he was
forced to quit or be dismissed for heavy drinking.
In civil life he failed to prosper, but the Civil War
rescued him from obscurity. Throwing himself
with immense energy into the raising and
training of volunteers, by August 1861 he was a
Brigadier General assigned to the Western
Theater.

Grant first attracted the eye of President
Lincoln and the press with the capture of Fort
Donelson in Tennessee in February 1862. At a
time of low morale in the Union Army, Grant's
widely reported insistence on the unconditional

surrender of the Fort's defenders was lauded. Two months later, fighting his first full-scale battle at Shiloh, he got a different type of press.

His camp was surprised and ambushed by Confederate forces while he was away, resulting in his army nearly being routed. Grant returned to seize control and managed to achieve an unlikely victory on the second day's fighting, but heavy Union losses shocked the Northern public. Tales of his heavy drinking circulated, but Lincoln kept faith in him, saying, "We can't spare this man: he fights".

Sidelined after Shiloh by his Theater Commander, General Henry Halleck, Grant contemplated quitting the Army but held on with moral support from General William T Sherman. By fall 1862, he was back in command and seeking a means to take the fortress of Vicksburg, the key to the Mississippi. Grant was a master of logistics, using river steamers and railroads to move troops and supplies. But in swampy terrain crawling with Confederate raiders, conventional maneuvers failed to succeed.

After months of frustration, in April 1863 Grant abandoned his link with a supply base and marched across country. Seizing Jackson, Mississippi, he kept in communication with the Federal forces who had been driven back into Vicksburg. After a six-week siege, Vicksburg surrendered and the Union had control of the Mississippi. The successes continued when he was later moved to Chattanooga in October, where a Union army was under siege after their defeat at Chickamauga. Grant brought in reinforcements, then took the initiative, opening the way for an advance into Georgia. In March 1864, Grant had the satisfaction of replacing Halleck as the Union General-in-Chief. Lincoln had recognized in him the man who could use the Union's superior force unflinchingly to grind down rebel resistance. Grant moved to the Eastern theater, using the trusted Sherman to run the Campaign in Georgia and Tennessee. Grant was in many ways a surprising person to mastermind the Union victory. He had surrounded himself with a personal staff of acquaintances from Illinois, men of no military training or distinction in civilian life, but whom he trusted and with whom he felt at ease. He hardly ever consulted his subordinate Commanders, running operations through a stream of clear, succinct orders written in his own hand. There was, in the words of one observer, "no glitter or parade about him". He made no flowery speeches – indeed, he never spoke to his troops at all – and usually wore a private's coat, going around with a cigar clenched between his teeth.

Grant's means of battling was equally sober and gritty. Convinced of the need of complete subjugation of the South through the destruction of its economic strength, he fully approved Sherman's scorched-earth approach for devastating the land in Georgia. He later ordered General Philip Sheridan to pursue the same policy in the Shenandoah Valley. His very own Overland campaign in Virginia in May and June 1864 was a relentless series of attacks on

Robert E. Lee's Army of Northern Virginia. He kept pressure on Lee regardless of cost, giving him no time to catch his breath. The slaughter at the bludgeoning battles of the Wilderness, Spotsylvania, and particularly Cold Harbor earned Grant a reputation as a butcher. Yet in his view there was no easier way to win the war.

The Overland campaign cost 55,000 Union casualties and failed to annihilate the Confederate Army, thanks to Lee's offensive ability. But it did impose losses on the Confederates that they could not afford and forced Lee to entrench around Petersburg. Grant played out the endgame implacably, yet showed generosity in the terms permitted to Lee upon his surrender.

Togo Heihachiro
Born: January 27, 1848

Died: May 30, 1934

Japanese Admiral

Togo Heihachiro was born into the Satsuma Samurai Clan in the port city of Kagoshima. As a youth, he saw the bombardment of Kagoshima by British vessels in 1863. The next year the Satsuma set out to create a modern Navy and Togo was among its very first volunteers. In 1868, he saw action in the Boshin War, a civil war in which the Satsuma fleet fought for Emperor Meiji against the Tokugawa Shogunate. After their victory, the Satsuma power became the foundation of the new Imperial Japanese Navy. In the 1870s, Togo was among many officials who were sent to Naval College in Britain. He developed a lifelong admiration of the customs of the Royal Navy and modeled himself on its hero, Horatio Nelson. When Japan later went to war with China in 1894, he was captain of a Cruiser. His sinking of a British-registered Transport Ship that was carrying Chinese troops caused a diplomatic uproar. Togo's appointment to command the Japanese Combined Fleet in 1903 was unexpected, but his leadership in the Russo-

Japanese war fully justified the choice. Following the initial surprise assault on Port Arthur, Togo blockaded the Russian First Pacific Squadron for six months. When the Russians attempted to bust out in August 1904, he inflicted heavy losses upon them in the battle of the Yellow Sea. His defeat of the Russian Baltic Fleet at Tsushima the following year won him worldwide renown.

Port Arthur

Admiral Togo planned to launch an assault on Port Arthur to neutralize the Russian Pacific Fleet before an official Declaration of War. He brought a Squadron of Destroyers to approach the port under cover of darkness and sink Russian warships in the harbor with torpedoes. The attack ended up being not as effectual as Togo intended. The Destroyer's formation became disturbed and only four participated in the first torpedo run, with others straggling behind. The brightly lit ships at anchor were an easy target, but they had been protected by torpedo nets. Three Russian warships were badly damaged, including their largest Battleship. The following morning, believing the Russian defense was crippled, Togo steamed his battle fleet toward Port Arthur, only to come under heavy fire from shore batteries and ships in harbor. Togo's flagship Mikasa was hit and the Japanese withdrew, settling instead for a lengthy blockade of the port.

Tsushima

On the night of May 26, 1905, Admiral Togo Heihachiro, commanding the Japanese Combined Fleet, had patrol ships strung along the Tsushima Strait. They were anxiously seeking the Russian warships bound for Vladivostok. Commanded by Admiral Zinovi Rozhdestvenski, the Russian fleet had sailed 18,000 miles from the Baltic to join the war against Japan's Pacific Fleet. Togo had traced their progress and was now waiting for their arrival in his home waters with all his vessels on full alert. He had guessed that when their supply of coal ran short, they would try to take a shortcut between Japan and Korea, rather than use the longer route to the east of Japan.

At 4:55 AM on May 27, Togo received the message he wanted. By the convenient medium of wireless telegraphy, the cruiser Shinano Maru informed him that they had made contact with the Russians. Informing Tokyo of the sighting, he stated that his Fleet would proceed forward to Tsushima to attack the adversary and destroy them. Throughout the next morning, Japanese Cruisers kept in contact with the Russian fleet, radioing updates to Togo as he hurried to give battle aboard his flagship Mikasa.

Togo was amazed at the convenience that radio systems provided. It allowed enemy movements and dispositions to be as clear to him (30 or 40 miles away) as if he were there himself. Later on, at around 1:40 PM, he established visual contact with the Russians. In conscious imitation of his hero, Admiral Nelson before the Battle of Trafalgar, Togo hoisted the Z flag on

Mikasa, a signal calling on every man to do his duty.

The Russian fleet was in poor shape after its long trip of steaming for six months. With ships capable of around 15 knots, Togo had complete freedom to engage when he wished. His initial choice of maneuver was recklessly daring. He attacked the Russian line with his flagship in the lead, and then performed a U-turn within range of the Russian guns. The Russians hit Mikasa, but their armor piercing shells had limited effect. It was very different from the Japanese rounds - designed to explode on contact – that rained down on the Russian ships. The Japanese gunners were better trained and had up-to-date rangefinders. Fired at 3.6 miles, their salvos were devastating. Rozhdestvenski's flagship Knyaz Suvorov was an early victim, the Admiral himself badly wounded. Swirling mist offered the Russians protection, but each time they were forced to exchange fire the end result was the same. The sinking of his battleship Borodino at around 7

PM was an apt conclusion to a battle that had ultimately decimated the Russian fleet. Togo withdrew his Battleships, unleashing his destroyers and torpedo boats to harass the Russians throughout the night. The next morning, Admiral Nikolai Nebogatov surrendered six Warships that were surrounded by Togo's Battle Fleet. Just three Russian ships ever reached Vladivostok. Togo claimed that the scale of the victory had been so great that his very own officers and men could find no language to express their astonishment. Seven Russian battleships, 4 cruisers, and 10 other ships were sunk with 4,380 men lost, compared to the Japanese losses of 3 torpedo ships and 117 men.

Chapter 6: Modern Combatants

John Monash

Born: June 27, 1865

Died: October 8, 1935

Australian General and Engineer

John Monash was a civil engineer who became a Militia Officer before 1914. He led a Brigade in the Anzac forces at Gallipoli in 1915. He was promoted to Command of a Division, and he trained his troops to a high standard of performance in England before taking them to the Western Front of World War I. Haig was impressed by Monash's performance in Flanders in 1917, especially at Messines Ridge. By May 1918, Monash was made Commander of the Australian Corps, which was at that time the largest Corps on the Western Front. He later played a vital role in recovering the town of Villers-Bretonneux after the German Army had overrun General Heneker's 8th British Division.

At Le Hamel in July 1918, Monash used massed machine gun infantry, tanks, artillery, and aircraft in a devastating lightning attack on a sector of the enemy line. It ended up being occupied by his infantry at little cost. He planned and coordinated combined-arms offenses to give maximum fire support to the advancing infantry.

This battle has since been described by historians as the "first modern battle" and it lasted only 93 minutes. British, American, and Australian troops all participated together, marking the first time in the War that American soldiers were left under an Allied General's command. Using tactics that were conventional for the period, it is believed that the fighting could have lasted for weeks or even months longer with significant additional casualties. By the end of the battle, 1,400 Allied soldiers were killed or wounded with 2,000 German soldiers killed and 1,600 captured. While the battle was small scale in comparison with other clashes of the war, it proved vital because it demonstrated firsthand superior tactics when engaging an entrenched enemy.

On a much larger scale, he employed the exact same tactics when his Australian forces spearheaded the Amiens offensive in August 1918. Overcoming the Hindenburg Line defenses at the St. Quentin's Canal in September was his last major action. General Monash stands out among his World War I contemporaries as an innovator. His example of combined-arms warfare would later become the battlefield standard in World War II, and continues to be relevant in the tactics of today.

Famously he later wrote, "...The true role of infantry was not to expend itself upon heroic physical effort, nor to wither away under merciless machine-gun fire, not to impale itself on hostile bayonets, nor to tear itself to pieces in hostile entanglements – but on the contrary, to advance under the maximum possible protection of the maximum possible array of mechanical resources, in the form of guns, machine-guns, tanks, mortars and aeroplanes; to advance with as little impediment as possible; to be relieved as far as possible of the obligation to fight their way forward; to march, resolutely, regardless of the din and tumult of battle, and to gather in the form of prisoners, guns and stores, the fruits of victory."

Erwin Rommel

Born: November 15, 1891

Died: October 14, 1944

German General

Erwin Rommel was the famous German General known as the "Desert Fox". The son of a school teacher, Erwin Rommel served as an Infantry Officer in World War I. His bravery in the line of fire resulted in his winning the coveted Pour le Merite decoration for gallantry. Additionally, he was awarded the Iron Cross for bravery after being wounded in the leg and then continuing to fight the French at great personal peril.

After the war, he assumed a teaching role like his father and grandfather before him, deciding to train others in infantry training and management at the War College until his brilliant tactical ideas, detailed in his 1937 book "Infantry Attacks", caught Hitler's attention. He was drawn into the Fuhrer's circle, taking command of his personal Security Battalion. Rommel had no experience with tanks, but his connection with Hitler resulted in command of the Seventh Armored Division in preparation of the invasion of France. It ended up being an inspired appointment, for Rommel spearheaded the breakneck advance from the Ardennes to the English Channel, emerging among the heroes of the triumphant campaign. Rommel's forces alone were responsible for capturing almost 100,000 French prisoners and 450 enemy tanks while only suffering losses of less than 42 tanks. His success was impossible to ignore.

In February 1941, he had been given command of the Afrika Corps, a force sent to North Africa to prevent the Italians from losing

Libya. He was soon promoted to Command of all Axis forces in the desert. He was characterized by his cunning and his willingness to lead his own troops from the front, often exposing himself to direct fire from the enemy. He was admired by his men for the same reasons as many great leaders of old – he would not ask them to do anything he was not willing to do himself.

Though starved of resources, Rommel outfoxed his British opponents, coordinating tank maneuvers that constantly caught his opponents unprepared. At Tobruk in 1942, his forces destroyed more than 250 British tanks from the British 8th Army and captured more than 30,000 prisoners of war.

The situation grew ever more tenuous and at one point he pleaded with Hitler for permission to evacuate his outnumbered men, and Hitler simply replied, "Victory or Death." Rommel understood that his troops were needed in defending Europe, but he had no option but to stay for the time being. Soon Rommel led his army on a 1,400 mile retreat while General Montgomery pursued him. His supplies continued to dwindle and with no support from Hitler, Rommel saw disaster approaching fast. After the inevitable disaster, Rommel was recalled from North Africa before the last Axis surrender.

He supervised the protection efforts of the French coast against Allied invasion, but was away on leave on D-Day. In July 1944, he was wounded in an air attack, which struck his car. Interestingly, there were two notable attempts on his life. On both occasions, small British commando units were sent to assassinate the General. Both attempts failed. After the failure of the first 'Rommel Raid', Rommel personally ordered a full military burial for the fallen British soldiers.

Although perhaps not a participant in the Hitler assassination plot, Rommel fell under suspicion and was forced by Hitler to commit suicide in order to avoid the trial and execution of his staff and family.

History has looked upon Rommel favorably and he is often seen as a good and chivalrous man who loved his people, his family, and his country but unfortunately served under a genocidal tyrant. He did not capitulate as many other German military leaders did. On multiple occasions he personally refused orders from Hitler if it conflicted with his strong sense of morality and justice. It is a testament to his valuable role in the German war effort that Rommel was not punished for these offenses when they occurred. He has been likened by many historians to Robert E Lee, the Confederate General in the American Civil War. His views did not reflect that of his leaders, but he fought out of a sense of duty.

His suicide was covered up on the direction of Hitler in order to instill a strong sense of nationalism at his tragic loss. It was publicly stated that he had died from his wounds sustained in the air attack in July 1944. Rommel was buried with full military honors and was survived by his wife, son, and daughter. His son

Manfred later became the Lord Mayor of
Stuttgart, Germany.

Georgy Zhukov
Born: December 1, 1896

Died: June 18, 1974

Soviet Marshal

Born into impoverishment, Georgy
Zhukov was conscripted into the Russian
Imperial Army in World War I. He fought for the
Bolsheviks in the Russian Civil War and made a
successful career as a Soviet officer. His trusted
position prevented him from death or dismissal
in Stalin's purges. In 1938, he commanded Soviet
soldiers fighting a border war against the
Japanese in Mongolia. In 1939, at Khalkhim Gol,
he crushed the Japanese troops with aggressive
use of tanks and motorized infantry. The prestige
gained in this war earned Zhukov the position of
Chief of the General Staff in January 1941. He
did not welcome the task, believing himself to be
a Field Commander rather than a Staff Officer.

He openly disagreed with Stalin's reaction to the German invasion and his insistence on no retreat. Zhukov was dismissed in July 1941, but remained one of the internal circle running the war. In September, he ended up being sent to hold Leningrad, which appeared to be close to falling to the enemy. In fact, the Germans did not attempt to take the city, but Zhukov appeared to have saved it. The next month, Stalin requested him to repeat the miracle at Moscow. German forces advancing on the capital were first halted and then in December, driven back with a well handled counter-offensive.

In October 1942, Stalin made Zhukov the Deputy Supreme Commander and ordered him to save Stalingrad. Operation Uranus, the offensive that cut off the German Army in the town, was systematically planned and rapidly and ruthlessly executed, showing Zhukov's skills at their best. In 1943, he masterminded the truly amazing Soviet triumph at Kursk. Operation Bagration, the massive Byelorussian offensive of the summer of 1944, showed how Zhukov along with other Soviet generals had learned the importance of combining all arms to smash through enemy defenses. This allowed them to maintain pressure across difficult terrain and against crushing opposition, no matter the cost in lives and material. Zhukov supervised the capture of Berlin in spring 1945 and ended the war as the most famous of Soviet Commanders. Soon demoted by a jealous Stalin, he returned for a time as Defense Minister in the 1950s.

Battle of Kursk

Zhukov resisted Soviet dictator Josef Stalin's idea for counterattacks that would have preempted the expected German offensive. Instead, Zhukov constructed formidable fortified lines, defended by minefields, entrenched infantry, anti-tank guns, and other artillery. He allowed the German tanks to exhaust themselves against these defenses before unleashing his armored reserves in a counterattack. Thanks to Soviet spies, Zhukov was informed of the place and timing of the German offensive. He was present at Rokossovsky's headquarters on the early morning of July 5, when Soviet artillery delivered a massive bombardment on German forces assembling for the assault. Over the next two days, Rokossovksy's defenses in the north held firm, but in the south German Armored forces threatened to break through.

On July 6, Zhukov ordered the 5th Guards Tank Army to advance from its reserve position 220 miles to the east. The T-34 tanks reached Prokhorovka on July 12 and plunged into battle with the Panzers, fighting them to a standstill in the largest armored encounter in history. More difficult battles were ahead, but the German offensive had been unsuccessful, and Zhukov was in a position to continue the offensive on a broader front.

Erich von Manstein, Commander of Army Group South, was responsible for the southern half of the operations at the Dell. The attack from the North was entrusted to Walter Model's Ninth Army, an element of Army Group Center. The two men disagreed over the operation and although Manstein was the most prestigious German general on the Eastern front, he had no authority over Model. Aware from aerial reconnaissance that the Soviets were constructing impressive defenses, Model concluded that an attack would play into the enemy's hands. Manstein – although he would have liked a subtler offensive – believed that the Dell provided an opportunity to inflict a crushing defeat on Soviet forces through a classic double envelopment. He knew, nevertheless, it must be performed quickly. It was not: after various delays, the operation was put back from an initial start date of May 3 to July 5. Manstein and Model adopted different tactics. While Model tried to clear paths through the minefields and trenches with his infantry before pushing his tanks forward, Manstein committed the concentrated armor of the Fourth Panzer Army and punched through the Soviet lines.

Winning air superiority at the beginning of the battle gave the Germans an inestimable advantage, but Soviet opposition was tougher than expected. By July 10, Model had reached the limits of his advance. Manstein did better, his Panzers plowing through the Soviet protective lines and swatting off counterattacks. Victory seemed within his grasp until July 12, when the completely unexpected arrival of Soviet armored reserves precipitated the tank battle at Prokhorovka. On July 13, Manstein was summoned to Hitler's headquarters where he argued against terminating the offensive. Model, however, was soon in complete retreat, eager to avoid encirclement as the Soviets opened a new offensive behind him at Orel. Manstein persisted, but by July 23, the Fourth Panzer Army had been driven back to its original starting position.

Bernard Montgomery

Born: November 17, 1887

Died: March 24, 1976

British Field Marshall

Bernard Law Montgomery was the son of the Anglican Bishop of Tasmania. His experience and leadership proved invaluable in leading a battered Britain through the chaos of the Second World War. Serving as a Staff Officer on the Western Front during World War I was a formative experience for him. Faced with the slaughter in the trenches, he became convinced that the whole point of war was to achieve your objective with as little loss of life as possible. It was to be achieved through meticulously planned combined arms operations executed by thoroughly trained troops that enjoyed superiority of numbers and gear.

After 1918, Montgomery saw some active service in Ireland as well as in Palestine, but most of his energies were focused on tactical training and military exercises. Although Montgomery's quarrelsome, opinionated nature frequently set him at odds with colleagues and superiors, he entered World War II as a divisional Commander. Sent to Europe, Montgomery ensured his Division was the best trained in the British Expeditionary Force. Scornful of the BEFs Commanders, he was well prepared for a rapid escape from Belgium and got his men home from Dunkirk without heavy losses. After keeping important positions in Britain, he was appointed to lead the Eighth Army in North Africa. The first choice, William Gott, died in an air crash.

Montgomery restored Army morale, making his presence known to the men through his natural showmanship. His long-held tactical views were vindicated at El Alamein, which was a victory that made him a national hero. However, the aftermath revealed Montgomery to be no master of mobile warfare, his sluggish maneuvers missing a chance to stop Rommel's retreat. The extension of the Desert war into Tunisia brought Montgomery another hard-fought victory in the taking of the Mareth Line.

He began working with the Americans, with whom relations were soon strained. In summer 1943, Allied amphibious landings in Sicily showcased Montgomery's skill at planning complex operations, yet American General George Patton then took delight in upstaging the British commander with his speed of movement in the conquest of the island. Montgomery's prestige remained high and he was given Command of all Allied land forces for the Invasion of Normandy in June 1944. Once again, his tactical judgment was vital in preparing for the landings, but once ashore his painfully slow struggle to take Caen drew American criticism. In September, the failure of Market Garden, an operation of uncharacteristic slowness, ended up being the worst setback of his career. Bad relations with American Generals came to a head at the Battle of the Bulge in the winter of 1944. There were complaints at US forces being placed under Montgomery's command, and resentment at his excessive claims of credit for the repulse for the German offensive. His methodical approach to crossing the Rhine in March 1945 further annoyed his allies, but casualties remained low. While occupying Northern

Germany, he accepted one of the German surrenders at Luneburg Heath.

Montgomery conceived Operation Market Garden to maintain the momentum of the Allied advance across France and Belgium. Airborne troops were to seize positions at Grave, Nijmegen, and Arnhem, while British armored forces dashed through to the Netherlands, crossing the bridges and threatening Northern Germany. United States Airborne Forces did take the very first two bridges, but at Arnhem, British parachute troops were trapped by SS Panzer Divisions. The armored advance was too slow to relieve the British troops, most of whom had been killed or were taken prisoner.

El Alamein

Bernard Montgomery took command of the British Eighth Army into the western desert on August 13, 1942. His task was to defeat Erwin Rommel's Panzerarmee Afrika, a German and Italian force that had repeatedly proved its mastery of desert combat. Montgomery's predecessor, Claude Auchinleck, had stopped Rommel's advance by taking a stand at El Alamein. After blocking a further Axis attack on August 31, Montgomery began preparations for a major offensive. Rommel – outnumbered two to one along with lengthy, vulnerable supply lines – founded a formidable defensive position fronted by minefields and waited for Montgomery to move.

Montgomery intended to win a definitive triumph by making superior force count against a more skillful enemy. He would attack the Axis forces where they were strongest and crumble their defenses until they broke and ran. Resisting demands from Prime Minister Winston Churchill for quick action, Montgomery delayed until he had incorporated reinforcements, including new American Sherman tanks, and improved the morale and training of his forces. According to Montgomery's program, the offensive would open with an artillery barrage. The infantry would then clear paths through the minefields under the cover of darkness, and tanks would advance down these lanes with the infantry and breaking through the enemy defenses. In practice, the barrage of October 23 worked, but the remainder did not. Mine clearing was too slow and traffic congestion blocked the cleared lanes. Still behind the infantry at daybreak, Tank Commanders refused to advance into the fire of German anti-tank guns. Despite reinforcing the line of attack and all Montgomery's urgings, by October 26 the offenses had become bogged down.

Churchill ended up being furious at the resulting lack of progress, but Montgomery kept his nerve. He understood that his army could afford the losses of attrition; if the British forces kept fighting they would win. While his front-line troops resisted furious Axis counterattacks, Montgomery organized a renewed offensive, code-named Supercharge. Skillfully varying the points of attack, he drove his army forward once again, insisting that tank formations be prepared to accept heavy casualties. Once the breakout came after 13 days of fighting, Montgomery failed to envelop Rommel's fleeing motorized forces. He ended up being content to mop up and consolidate after a hard-won triumph.

Withdrawn from the desert on sick leave, Rommel might never have returned to Africa but for the death of his replacement, General Stumme, on the first early morning of the battle. Even then Hitler hesitated to send him back – Rommel spent the nights October 24-25 at an airport in Vienna awaiting the Fuhrer's orders. It was finally confirmed on October 25 once the Axis forces at El Alamein received the crisp message: "I have taken over the Army again. Rommel."

Rommel's forte was aggressive mobile warfare but Montgomery had him trapped in static defense. To regain the initiative, Rommel tried to move his tanks rapidly to wherever in the line Montgomery was pressing and land powerful counter blows. But his supply situation was critical. Every redeployment needed to be weighed in terms of the fuel it required. He lacked air cover, and this meant his formations could not travel by day without being decimated by the RAF. Armored counterattacks on a restricted battlefield packed with enemy tanks and antitank guns proved exceedingly costly.

As early as October 29, Rommel began planning a withdrawal to the west. His official communications with Axis headquarters in Rome – made open to Montgomery by the British code breakers – consisted of a stream of appeals for even more fuel and ammunition. His private letters to his spouse unveiled a fatalistic, death obsessed state of mind. On November 2nd, he judged the situation untenable and ordered a withdrawal. Hitler countered with a stand fast order, demanding victory or death. Rommel felt he had to send an envoy to explain the situation to Hitler face-to-face. In the end, Hitler's intervention only delayed the retreat by one day. Once on the retreat with his tanks – abandoning the Italian non motorized infantry – the Desert Fox returned to form. He outpaced his enemies in the race westward, eventually reaching the

Tunisian border, ready to fight again the following year.

George Patton

Born: November 11, 1885

Died: December 21, 1945

U.S. Army General

A polarizing figure, General George Patton was simultaneously dreaded and highly regarded by Allied and German commanders alike. He additionally earned the esteem of his men, who, when asked later on where they served, would merely reply, "I was with Patton". Following education at the US Military Academy West Point, Patton served as an officer in a Cavalry Regiment. He subsequently received attention, within the Army as the creator of a new cavalry sword, and to the wider public as a competitor in the modern pentathlon in the 1912 Olympic games. His very first active service was in the US intervention in Mexico in 1916 to 1917. During the course of this conflict, Patton was involved in a well-publicized shootout with a bandit leader.

Patton next saw effective service as one of his country's earliest Tank Officers in France in World War I. Perpetually an avid student of military history and theory, Patton was quick to understand that Germany's developments in tank warfare would have to be taken up in the United States Armed Forces. With the expansion of the U.S. Army that began in 1940, Patton consequently decided to leave his beloved Cavalry for the recently established Armored Corps. His success in training cutting edge tank units marked him out for greater command.

In November 1942, Patton led the Western Task Force in Operation Torch, the Anglo-American invasion of Northwest Africa. His command saw minimal fighting, but, in March 1943, he was called to the front in Tunisia, where he took over the under performing US II Corps, transforming it with his vigor and determination. A ferocious disciplinarian, Patton always insisted on his men being dressed in correct uniforms. He also cultivated an inspiring presence, regularly visiting forward units and imbuing his speeches to the troops with a charisma that transcended his surprisingly high-pitched voice. Although in private he could be sensitive and thoughtful, his public speech was adorned with obscenities and combative, bloodthirsty remarks.

It was during the Tunisian campaign that Patton first came across the British General Bernard Montgomery. The pair would have a complicated partnership marked, on Patton's side, by an intense sense of competition. In general, Patton found it hard to work with British Commanders, becoming paranoid that the US Armed Forces were being belittled and manipulated by their British allies. The Germans and Italians in Tunisia surrendered in May 1943, and the following month Patton was awarded charge of Seventh Army for the invasion of Sicily. The invasion was a triumph, but controversy endangered Patton's career. His exhortations to kill Germans were cited in the defense of soldiers who had murdered prisoners, and he was accused of striking two hospitalized soldiers whom he accused of malingering. Allied Commander-in-Chief, Dwight D. Eisenhower, intervened, recognizing that Patton was valuable to the war effort and instructed him to make amends. Eisenhower then sent Patton to Britain in December as part of a plan manufactured to confound the Germans about the location and timing of the D-Day landings.

In January 1944, Patton took command of the Third Army, which would play a leading role in the Allied breakout from the Normandy beachhead following the D-Day landings. The Third Army's advance across France to the German border in August 1944 was impressive and brought Patton acclaim, but when the German defenses stiffened, he struggled to organize his forces for effective assaults. Patton's finest hour was unquestionably his role in the Battle of the Bulge. In this, along with the final defeat of Germany in the spring of 1945, he showed that he was truly an expert of rapid maneuver. Patton was made Armed Forces Governor of Bavaria at the end of the war, but – controversial to the last – he was formally relieved of Command at the beginning of October 1945 after failing to follow de-Nazification policies. He was fatally injured in a car accident in Germany just over two months later.

Battle of the Bulge

When the previously calm Ardennes sector erupted on December 16, 1944, with a sizable German assault – the last significant German offensive of World War II – the top Allied commanders were taken by surprise. The German army smashed into a line held by a weak mix of exhausted veterans and newcomers from General Courtney Hodges US First Army. Allied defenses were eventually broken, although some units (such as the 101st Airborne) did manage to hold on at St. Vith and Bastogne. In the hilly and heavily wooded landscapes of the Ardennes, the road networks that spread out from these communities were vital.

The Germans were by no means likely to accomplish their goal of reaching Antwerp in the Northwest, but the gaps they were creating in the Allied front line was a serious danger. It was only on December 19 that Allied leaders began to take action successfully. At a planning conference, General Eisenhower decided that north of the Bulge, Bernard Montgomery would be responsible for the halting of the German advance and in counterattacking. Omar Bradley was given the corresponding duty to the south, but, in effect, George Patton, commanding the US Third Army, became the driving force behind the southern operations. At Eisenhower's conference, officers were disbelieving when Patton claimed that he could have three Divisions on the attack against the German southern flank – some 90 miles from their existing position – within 48 hours. But Patton made it work. Over the next few days, Patton alone worked at the Third Army's forward headquarters, writing from unit to unit in hurrying all of them along the line of march, adjusting their deployment, and, finally, sending them into combat. The relief of Bastogne was completed on December 26, and on January 16 the Third Army linked up at Houffalize with forces of Hodges' First Army striking from the north.

Patton's forces did not win the Battle of the Bulge on their own. Even as he got his men moving, other American infantry in tank units were converging on the sector from all sides. But as a feat of leadership, Patton's achievement in planning and executing the Third Army's attack has few equals in any conflict. The German attack had been a painful risk that did not pay off.

Other books available by author on Kindle, paperback and audio

Hannibal Barca, The Greatest General: The Meteoric Rise, Defeat, and Destruction of Rome's Fiercest Rival

The Rise and Fall of the Roman Empire: Life,
Liberty, and the Death of the Republic

Made in the USA
San Bernardino, CA
28 February 2018